William Verplanck, Moses Collyer
The Sloops of the Hudson

William Verplanck, Moses Collyer

The Sloops of the Hudson

ISBN/EAN: 9783954272129
Erscheinungsjahr: 2012
Erscheinungsort: Bremen, Deutschland

© maritimepress in Europäischer Hochschulverlag GmbH & Co. KG, Fahrenheitstr. 1, 28359 Bremen. Alle Rechte beim Verlag und bei den jeweiligen Lizenzgebern.

www.maritimepress.de | office@maritimepress.de

Bei diesem Titel handelt es sich um den Nachdruck eines historischen, lange vergriffenen Buches. Da elektronische Druckvorlagen für diese Titel nicht existieren, musste auf alte Vorlagen zurückgegriffen werden. Hieraus zwangsläufig resultierende Qualitätsverluste bitten wir zu entschuldigen.

THE SLOOPS OF THE HUDSON

THE "HALF MOON" ON THE HUDSON

From the painting by L. W. Seavey in State Capitol, Albany

THE
SLOOPS OF THE HUDSON

AN HISTORICAL SKETCH OF THE PACKET AND MARKET
SLOOPS OF THE LAST CENTURY, WITH A RECORD
OF THEIR NAMES; TOGETHER WITH PER-
SONAL REMINISCENCES OF CERTAIN
OF THE NOTABLE NORTH RIVER
SAILING MASTERS

BY

WILLIAM E. VERPLANCK

AND

MOSES W. COLLYER

ILLUSTRATED

IRA J. FRIEDMAN, INC.
Port Washington, Long Island, N.Y.

PREFACE

No history of the sloops of the Hudson, so far as I can learn, has ever been written, nor has any more than a bare reference here and there been made to them in the literature of the past sixty years.

Cooper and Irving make mention of these useful vessels, and in a way that makes it quite evident that their importance in the daily life of the people struck the imagination of those writers in a lively manner. But later writers have apparently ignored the sloop. Perhaps, it was because she was like those worthy persons who make no noise as they go through the world and whose quiet and useful lives are taken as a matter of course.

The sloop was the forerunner in the establishment of the vast commerce of the Hudson which has now reached an extent that

Preface

is exceeded by few, if any, rivers in the world, and as this vessel played so important a part in the development and growth of the State of New York, particularly in connection with the Erie Canal, causing the city of New York to rise to be the chief city of the United States, it seems quite fitting that something should be written to preserve the memory of these inland merchantmen.

The steamboats of the Hudson beginning with the *Clermont* have been described and catalogued both in popular and technical style in compliance with the wishes of the reading public, so it occurred to me that a book on the sloops might also be a warrantable venture on the sea of literature. If some critic insists that such books are in great part mere lists of names of vessels long since gone to oblivion, then I retort that Homer had his "Catalogue of the Ships."

My acquaintance with sloops goes back to my early boyhood when I began sailing a skiff with a leg-o'-mutton sail. My home

Preface

was on the east shore of Newburgh bay, and a capital place for sailing it is. Sloops and schooners then were constantly passing the house, frequently as many as twenty-five in a day, and often they would lie at anchor off our place for hours at a time waiting for a change of tide. It was then that I would sail out, and by one pretext or another manage to get aboard. Perhaps, baskets of apples or cherries made it easier to cross the gunwale. In this way I got to know several of the skippers or captains, and soon learned to tell the vessels apart at a distance. I had my favorite sloops and hated to see them outsailed or looking shabby as was sometimes the case. The proudest day of my life was when Captain Geo. Woolsey of the *Samsondale* gave me the tiller, and I called out "Hard-a-lee" to the man at the jib, as I put the sloop on the other tack.

A great event in my life was a voyage to Albany with Capt. John Bradley, of Low Point, in his sloop *J. L. Richards*. I was then twelve years old, and several boys of my own age were in the party, the captain's son among them. The river was teeming with sturgeon in those days—big fellows weighing 250 lbs. would be seen leaping several feet into the air, and now and then one would fall on the deck. The catching and packing of these fish was then an important industry along the Hudson. The product was known as "Albany beef," but, owing to its cheapness and abundance, it was disdained as a food, albeit the flavor and nutriment, when well prepared, were of a high order. We were gone a week and I well remember that we lay at anchor two days off Coeymans waiting for the south wind, with several other vessels, for the flood-tides were weak, and we thought the tugs demanded too much to tow us to Albany, twelve miles farther up the river.

Later in my career as the possessor in turn of a catboat and of a twenty-eight-foot sloop,

Preface

I took part in the many regattas which occurred on Newburgh bay. Mr. Irving Grinnell of New Hamburgh with the *Fidget* and Judge Charles F. Brown of Newburgh with the *Lorelei*, were leading spirits on these occasions. Nor should the Van Wyck brothers of New Hamburgh with their *Bonita* be forgotten.

In collecting the material for my part of this book, I have had much assistance from my old friend, Capt. Moses W. Collyer of Chelsea (formerly Low Point), and he has been several years gathering facts for his part. With him I have spent much time on the water and on the ice, too, for that matter, from the days when he began his career as a mere lad on the Sloop *Benj. Franklin* with his father, the late John L. Collyer, a brother of Thomas Collyer of steamboat fame.

Capt. Moses Collyer has had an experience of over forty years on the River and the Sound, as captain and owner successively of sloop, schooner, steam barges and lighters. He has been faithful and consistent in following the water, and has very justly prospered in so doing.

WILLIAM E. VERPLANCK.

FISHKILL-ON-HUDSON,
  September, 1908.

CONTENTS.

PART		PAGE
I.—THE SLOOP AS A PACKET VESSEL.		1
II.—THE SAIL IN COMPETITION WITH STEAM		76
III.—PERSONAL REMINISCENCES OF CAPTAIN GEORGE D. WOOLSEY		112

ILLUSTRATIONS

FACING PAGE

THE "HALF MOON" ON THE HUDSON
Frontispiece
From the painting by L. W. Seavey in State Capitol, Albany.

A TYPICAL HUDSON RIVER SLOOP . . 2
From a painting by W. Sheppard. Reproduced from "The Rudder" by permission of The Rudder Publishing Co., New York.

SCHOONER "WM. A. RIPLEY," FORMERLY OWNED BY ROBERT COLLYER OF CHELSEA 38
From an old photograph.

THE PALISADES OF THE HUDSON . . 50
From a photograph by W. J. Wilson.

CAPTAIN JOHN PAYE OF FISHKILL . . 52
From a photograph by Cramer, Matteawan, N. Y.

CAPTAIN AUGUSTUS WESLEY HALE, LATE OF SAUGERTIES 58
From a photograph by Austin.

CAPTAIN MARTIN V. DRAKE OF NEW HAMBURGH, N. Y. 66
From a photograph by the Benedict Studios, New York.

xii   Illustrations

FACING PAGE

SLOOP "MARY DALLAS". . . . 68
    Owned by Captain Martin V. Drake of New Hamburgh. From an oil painting owned by him.

CAPTAIN MOSES WAKEMAN COLLYER OF CHELSEA 76
    From a photograph by Whitney, Poughkeepsie, N. Y.

SLOOP "BENJAMIN FRANKLIN" WITH CAPTAIN JOHN L. COLLYER ON THE DECK 82
    From a photograph taken at Seabring's dock, Low Point, 1881.

THE SCHOONER "IRON AGE," CAPTAIN JOHN PINCKNEY OF LOW POINT, NOW CHELSEA 92
    From an oil painting.

CAPTAIN JOHN LYON COLLYER, LATE OF LOW POINT 102
    From a photograph by F. E. Walker, Fishkill-on-Hudson.

CAPTAIN GEORGE DAVIS WOOLSEY, LATE OF NEWBURGH 112
    Reproduced from an old print.

SLOOP "GENERAL PUTNAM," BUILT BY CHARLES COLLYER 168
    From an oil painting.

THE SLOOPS OF THE HUDSON

The Sloops of the Hudson

PART I

THE SLOOP AS A PACKET VESSEL[1]

THE three hundredth anniversary of the discovery of the Hudson, soon to be celebrated with the centenary of Fulton's success in steam navigation, serves to direct the attention to that river, and its commerce.

Between the *Half Moon* and the *Clermont* there were two centuries, and it was during that period that the North River sloop was developed and perfected. The Hudson, let it be said in passing, became known in early colonial times as the North River to distinguish it from the Delaware or South River.

The sloop proved so useful a vessel, that

[1] Written by William E. Verplanck.

Sloops of the Hudson

it is only within the past twenty years that she has passed away. The sloop died not directly because of the *Clermont* and her successors,—those giant steam passenger boats that now ply between New York and Albany,—but she succumbed, with the schooner, rather to the great steam drawn "Tows" that now pass slowly and silently up and down the river bearing on their barges, scows and canal boats the vast tonnage that makes up the commerce of the river. The sloops did not feel the competition of the early steamboats, and in fact often made better time between Albany and New York, when the wind was fair; nor at first did the sloops appear to have difficulty in withstanding the competition of the towboat companies, but when they were combined to meet the great increase in the size and number of cargoes, necessitating vessels of larger tonnage to transport the commodities to the New York markets with reasonable despatch and regularity, then the sailing vessels of the Hudson were doomed. They

A TYPICAL HUDSON RIVER SLOOP

From a painting by W. Sheppard and reproduced from *The Rudder* by permission of The Rudder Publishing Co., New York

The Packets

made a good fight, however, and with their defeat has disappeared one of the most picturesque features of the Hudson River.

The sail is rarely seen on the river to-day, except here and there a small schooner, catboat, or other yacht, and the larger sailing yachts that twenty years ago passed up and down have been superseded by the steam yacht or motor boat. Even the occasional yacht will use her "auxiliary" instead of spreading her sails. The Hudson is fast becoming a canal, as the Rhine has already become, with double-track railways on both banks and twenty factory chimneys to one castle. The width of the Hudson is however sufficient to hide or obscure many of the ugly objects that now line the shore.

The sloop, as its name indicates, is of Dutch origin. They called her a *sloëp*. It is the same word as the French *chalupe*, and the Portuguese *chalupa*. In its simplest form, it is a vessel of one mast, carrying a mainsail, jib, and generally a topsail, Additional jibs and other sails are, of course, carried on yachts. The sloop differs from the cutter, and other one-masted "fore-and-aft" vessels in having her bowsprit fixed, while with the cutter it can be drawn in or "housed." The cutter is narrow, deep, and sharp and has a keel. For steering the sloop a long tiller was used instead of the wheel which was not introduced until later.

The Dutch settlers of New Netherland, as well as the English and French, who soon merged with them, saw the advantages of the sloop rig for the commerce of the river and the Sound. At first she was fitted with "lee boards" after the fashion of Holland where they still linger. But the advantage of the centre board, or shifting keel, for shoal water and sailing to windward was soon introduced, perhaps from England, where the device is known as the "drop keel."

The sloops of the Hudson were about of the same size, say one hundred tons' capacity and about 65 to 75 feet in length. They were full forward, like the other Dutch

The Packets

vessels, and had a high quarter-deck, which is a survival of the poop-decks of the medieval vessels. The mast was placed well forward, thus giving the boat a large mainsail, and small jib. A topsail too was generally carried, but not set like the club topsail of the modern yacht. The quarter-deck afforded space for the cabin accommodations for the passengers of the packet sloops, many of which before the days of steamboats were fitted up as such, and carried no bulky freight, only parcels, letters, etc. There was an ample deck for promenade or dancing, so altogether the packet sloop was far from being an uncomfortable means of conveyance. The packets held the river for many years. I have family letters in which mention is frequently made of the sloops showing that they were a favorite means of travel and for shipping light articles, parcels, and letters.

Some of the letters are given below:

Miss Mary Walton writing from New York under date of October 16, 1806, to her sister, Mrs. Daniel C. Verplanck at Fishkill, says:

MY DEAR SISTER:
I was very happy to hear by DeLancey that you had so good a passage up—and that you found all well at Mount Gulian. He got back to the old mansion [the Walton House on Franklin Square] about 11 o'clock on Sunday night; not expecting him before Monday all hands were gone to Bed. I had just put out my Candle when he knocked at the door. I regretted you hurried away last friday, so did old Abby who came back from the Sloop a few minutes after you left me. She expected to meet you and tell you the Sloop was not to go till 2 o'clock. I suppose you had stopped at the Booksellers which made her miss you. She carried your slippers on board & put them in your Basket. Beautiful weather again this week I walked out to Nut Shell Hall yesterday afternoon and found the three Sisters together. . . . I have not heard from Heathcote Hall since you left me—I must write to Mrs. De Lancey soon. Mrs. Quick & Mrs. Van Wagenen sent me word this Minute they would take tea with me this afternoon—I will leave my letter to finish in the evening.—My party are just gone. Henrietta Hook came with her sister. Mr. Quick came to tea, but the other Benedicts did

not make their appearance till the Tea Table was removed. I treated them with Pears and Grapes and we were very social. Nothing occurred in conversation to put in my letter except Mrs. Quick's saying you made her very happy by staying to dine with her. She desired her best regards to you. . . . . Charlotte Ogden was shopping the other day & met Mrs. Cooper with her son Tom—She stopped & said to her what fine relations I have. They scarcely know if I am alive or not— I have begun Housekeeping a very short distance from Dey Street. Mrs. O. told her she was only in Town for a few hours. Should not move in till the last of the month—She talks of calling to see Mrs. C. as she must pass the House so frequently. Grace L. said she was afraid to visit her as she might have more of Mrs. C.'s good company than was agreeable. She has heard how well Charlotte O. lives & makes advances to be noticed by her. Joanna wants to lounge where something good is to be got. No one can assume affability better than our cousin Mrs. C. when she pleases. Her jaunt to Virginia did not mend her Health as she expected—had a bad turn there without making a misgo,—is in a Family way—she breeds like a Rabbit. Grace R. is a woman. . . . Maria R. is well but subject to those strange sensations that she had last winter. Mrs. O. wished you could have spent a day at the Nut Shell with her. . . . I drank tea with Uncle G. on Sunday, went twice to Church. . . . Did you think of telling Helen, Abby saw her Husband & gave him her letter?—She has not seen him since. The old woman went to the Bishop this afternoon to be christened—her mind will be easy now. . . . God bless and preserve you in Health with those most dear to you, my dear Sister is the fervent prayer of

Your truly affectionate sister
MARY WALTON

P. S. Abby's respects & her regards to Helen. My love to Mrs. Dewint and the girls.

This letter folded and sealed in the fashion of the day before the invention of envelopes was forwarded by sloop to Fishkill, and this was the year before the *Clermont* made her first trip. The address on the letter has this note "To the care of Capt<u>n</u> A. Weeks with a Pot & Basket."

James DeLancey Walton[1] writing to his sister at Fishkill, September 8, 1826, sends the letter "care of A. Davids, Sloop *Caroline*, with a Basket." He says:

[1] He was a warden of St. George's Church, the first independent offshoot from Trinity.—W. E. V.

The Packets

MY DEAR NANCY:

I have packed your medicine in the Basket with the Sweet Potatoes—The Bark and Rhubarb I had put in bottles. . . . Gulian dined and went to the funeral of Judge Van Ness. I had to go to the Steam Boat to forward a letter covering one from Walton. Neither of the Mail Boats were there and I gave it to the Captain of the *Sandusky* who promised to send it on shore at Newburgh. I hope he will not take it on to Albany. . . . The Morewoods, Lydes and Ogdens were all well yesterday. . . . Tell Mary her old acquaintance Charlotte White called to pay her a Visit with her sister Amelia. *She* was well made up and both were smartly dressed.

On July 8th of the same year he wrote his sister from New York "care of Capt. A. Davids, Sloop *Caroline* with a Box & Basket." He says:

I bought a box of spermaceti Candles and put them on board the *Caroline* yesterday afternoon with a Basket of Crackers which were all the commissions for this week. . . . I found it very warm in the Market and walking in the Streets, have a hot walk to take to the Sloop with the letter, and if Davids was as punctual in leaving the City as he is from the Long Dock

[Fishkill] I shall have my walk for nothing. . . .
Mr. Adams is Dead and there is a report of the death of Mr. Jefferson this morning.

The same Mr. Walton writing to his young niece at Fishkill, September 9, 1825 says:

"I am much gratified on receiving your letter announcing your safe arrival with your aunt. . . . If the weather will permit and I can meet with suitable Fruit I will send it by the Sloop. . . . Mrs. Lagrange has not sent home your Corsette; if it comes in time I will forward it. . . . Miss Van Ness & her Brother called—a Visit intended for your Ladyship—supposing you still in the City. . . .

P. S. I send two Baskets of Peaches & 1 of Damsons. I have picked them over carefully to try & preserve them. Your Corsettes were Brought Home just in time to be put in the Box with the Shoes.

On July 22, 1824, Mr. Walton writes to his sister at Fishkill and sends the letter "care of Capt. T. Brett, Sloop *Levant* with a trunk."

July 16, 1824, he writes her again:

I wrote a few lines to send by the *Boxer* with a Demijohn of Brandy. I could not find a man that I was acquainted with to take it to the Sloop. I now send it by the *Belvidere*, Capt. J. Wiltse.

Here is an account of a trip by sloop in early winter, written from Fishkill.

MY DEAR MARY:
. . . I arrived here yesterday between the hours of four & five and found all the family well from Mamma and Aunt to Goliath and Cherry. I had a very pleasant passage notwithstanding my melancholy forebodings, which, had they been yours, would doubtless have been realized. The weather was sufficiently mild to allow us to remain on deck, at first. For about thirty miles we met with large cakes of ice, but after we entered the Highlands we met with none to impede our progress. I think I never admired the scenery of the North river so much as I did yesterday; the water was as smooth as glass and reflected the mountains as distinctly as a mirror, and the mountains themselves covered with snow presented a much more imposing effect than in summer—We landed first at the Long dock, as we had on board some bales of cotton for Matteawan—Phil, whose gallantry would hardly suffer him to allow me to ride two miles alone, went on shore to look for a safe and sober driver, and finding Mr. Rogers there,

he asked him to take me home, which Mr. Rogers very politely consented to do—See! how easy it is for a poor helpless maiden to travel alone.

Travellers from New England even made use of the sloops to reach New York by way of Poughkeepsie. They would travel across the country on the Dutchess Turnpike, a famous road of past days running from Northern Connecticut through Dutchess county to Poughkeepsie and there embark for New York. The diary of Samuel Miles Hopkins, who came from Litchfield, Conn. in 1791 to practise law in New York, states: "I embarked at Poughkeepsie on the good sloop, *John Jay* and soon saw the wonderful city, the compact parts of which extend to St. Paul's Church and then up Chatham Street to the Tea Water Pump, or nearly." The *John Jay* kept the river as late as 1865.

Frequently, better time was made by the sloop than by the stage-coach, particularly in the summer months, on the passage to Albany

The Packets

when the south wind prevailed. The packet sloops held their own until the steamboats were perfected which was some time after the *Clermont*. She was slow, and did not disdain to carry a sail, and the sloops and schooners had no difficulty in passing her when running before the wind when a speed of eight to ten miles an hour was attained. The sloop *Caroline* once sailed from New York to Fishkill a distance of sixty miles in five hours. She was built about 1820, by the late John Peter De Wint, Esq., of Fishkill and named in honor of his daughter, who married A. J. Downing, the originator of landscape architecture in the United States. While such a run was unusual, if not unprecedented, yet it was often approached by other sloops of the early part of the last century. In tacking or sailing against the wind, the sloops did good work and a speed of five to six miles an hour was often reached, when the tide was favorable. Though considerable "sea" is kicked up when the tide and wind are in opposite directions, it was rarely enough to retard the larger sailing vessels. The sloops too could "beat" to windward against the tide when there was a fresh breeze. But as a rule, when the wind and tide were unfavorable they lay at anchor until the tide turned, as it does every six hours.

As the tide plays an important part in the navigation of the Hudson a few words on the subject may not be amiss. Now the Hudson is an estuary or arm of the sea, and the tidal influence extends as far up as the State dam at Troy, above which the river, properly so called, may be said to begin. In the lower part of the Hudson, and particularly at New York where filling in and new piers on both shores have narrowed the original stream by half a mile, the tide reaches a speed of over three miles per hour, while at Tappan Zee, where the river is nearly four miles wide the speed is much lower. I refer to both flood- and ebb-tides. At Hudson, which is about one hundred and twenty miles up the river,

The Packets

I have seen the flood-tide rush past the docks at a lively rate, which made it hard to tack against. But this was during the dry summer season when the Hudson's tributaries were low. During the spring freshets of the upper Hudson and Mohawk, the flood-tide is checked in its movement northward for thirty to forty miles below Albany, so that the effect of the flood-tide pressing upward from the ocean is merely to raise the level of the surface of the river. Further down, say from Kingston southward, the flood-tide seems to run at all seasons nearly as fast as the ebb. The effect of the salt water from the sea is completely neutralized at Poughkeepsie by the fresh water from above, and, there the city pumps the water from the river into reservoirs for the general use of the inhabitants.

The skippers, or sailing masters, of the sloops well understood the tide and its vagaries, and there are many. They knew how to use them when favorable and how to avoid their adverse effects. For instance the flood-tide will "make" on some reaches of the river, nearly an hour earlier on one shore than on the other, and again, the ebb will "hang on" in certain parts of the river longer than another. Nor does the tide always run up and down parallel to or following the trend of the shore line. It glances at the end of a reach just after the river turns, thus causing the current to be deflected toward the opposite bank at an angle of nearly forty-five degrees. The pilots of the steamboats also take advantage of these eccentricities, crossing and recrossing the river several times on a trip between Albany and New York.

I once lost a race in a regatta on Newburgh bay in not fully knowing the local tide movement. The yachts were beating down to the lower stake boat against a good breeze on the ebb-tide. There was quite a sea running in which my boat was at her best but I knew that a good lead was necessary, as the second boat was faster than mine running before the wind. I turned well

The Packets

ahead of the others, and squared away to run home before the wind, confident of winning, but quite ignoring the direction of the tide current and thus lost the race, for the boat, second at the stake, followed a course while somewhat longer, yet thereby avoided the strength of the ebb, and passed the mark well in the lead.

There is another peculiarity of the tide—while it may reach a speed of even four miles an hour at flood or ebb, the tide "crest" moves at the rate of about fifteen miles an hour. For example when it is high water at New York at noon, it will be high water at Newburgh, sixty miles up the river, at four o'clock, so that a fast steamboat can and does for many weeks, at intervals varying with the moon's tidal influence, carry the flood-tide all the way to Albany; and again, the same boat may have the ebb-tide to contend with throughout the whole of her nine-hour trip from New York to Albany. Thus, as the boat proceeds up the river at the rate of say fifteen miles an hour she keeps in the same stage of the tide with its retardation of about an hour for every fifteen miles up stream. The trip down the river, on the other hand, gives quite dissimilar results, for then a steamboat and even a sailing vessel, running before the wind, will encounter a different tide about every four hours. Suppose, for instance, the boat left Albany on the middle of the ebb, by the time Catskill was reached the flood would be met, owing to the earlier time of high water there, and so, as the vessel passed down the river always going to meet the tide as it were, the ebb would again be running long before the expiration of six hours. The result of this is that the steamboats of the Day Line between New York and Albany, which make the trip in about nine hours, encounter but one tide on the way up and three on the way down.

When it is high water at New York it is low water at Kingston; when on Newburgh bay the flood is running at full strength,

The Packets

at Albany it is high water. The tide continues to run up for more than an hour after high water and to run down after low water for about the same period. In this respect the Hudson is like other estuaries.

So much for the tide, and without it sail-navigation on the Hudson would be quite another affair, and the voyage to Albany might indeed have taken a week or more in old times, as one is told was often the case. Perhaps Irving is responsible for this error as he was for others in regard to the early history of New York, because his facetious *Diedrich Knickerbocker* seems to have been taken seriously by many of its early readers. All that concerned the Hudson was of great interest to him, and naturally the sloops came under observation. In *Dolph Heyliger* the departure of one of them for Albany is thus described:

He [Dolph] was unconsciously carried along by the impulse of the crowd, and found it was a sloop on the point of sailing up the Hudson to Albany. There was much leavetaking, and kissing of old women and children, and great activity in carrying on board baskets of bread and cakes and provisions of all kinds, notwithstanding the mighty joints of meat that dangled over the stern; for a voyage to Albany was an expedition of great moment in those days. . . . I have said that a voyage up the Hudson in those days was an undertaking of some moment; indeed it was as much thought of as a voyage to Europe is at present. The sloops were often many days on the way; the cautious navigators taking in sail when it blew fresh, and coming to anchor at night, and stopping to send the boat ashore for milk for tea, without which it was impossible for the worthy old lady passengers to subsist, and there were the much talked of perils of the Tappaan Zee, and the Highlands. In short a prudent Dutch burgher would talk of such a voyage for months, and even years, beforehand; and never undertook it without putting his affairs in order, making his will, and having prayers said for him in the Low Dutch Churches, . . . On the second day of the voyage they came to the Highlands.

The last paragraph is somewhat surprising, for the author previously tells us that the sloop sailed early in the morning with a spanking breeze and favorable tide, and soon was "ploughing her way past Spiking Devil and Yonkers, and the tallest chimneys of the Manhattoes had faded from his [Dolph's] view." Such a tide and breeze would have carried the slowest of sloops as far as Kingston by sundown, unless, of course, there were detentions caused by the "old lady passengers" sending ashore for milk. Later on in the story we are told that the Highlands were thought

to be under the dominion of supernatural and mischievous beings which seemed to have taken some pique against the Dutch colonists. In consequence of this they have ever taken particular delight in venting their spleen and indulging their humors upon the Dutch skippers, bothering them with flaws, head winds, counter-currents and all kinds of impediments insomuch that a Dutch navigator was always obliged to be exceedingly wary and deliberate in his proceedings; to come to anchor at dusk, to drop his peak or take in sail whenever he saw a swagbellied cloud rolling over the mountains; in short to take so many precautions that he was apt to be an incredible time in toiling up the river.

The evidence is quite convincing of the

fast time that the sloops actually made in the voyages up and down the river. By taking the tide on the first of the flood with a good south wind, and leaving the Battery at, say six o'clock A.M., the vessel would be in Newburgh bay at noon, and at Poughkeepsie by two and Hudson at eight or nine. Unless the wind failed at sundown, which is often the case for an hour or so, rising afterwards, Albany would be reached easily early the next morning, or twenty-four hours from the time of leaving. This run has been made in less time.

As the south wind is apt to prevail in summer the return trip would experience headwinds, and assuming there were no calms, the sloop could easily be back in New York at the end of four days, and in seven if calms prevailed most of the time. But it is very rare, if indeed it ever happens, that there is no breeze at any time of day or night. The sloops sailed at night, unless the weather were thick, and took advantage of every turn of the tide.

The Packets

From Cooper, too, we learn much of the history of the days of the sloops, and he is always more accurate than Irving is, without being any the less interesting. Now Cooper was a seaman, having served for several years in the navy Besides he had practical knowledge of the navigation of the Hudson and its sailing craft. I quote from *Afloat and Ashore*, chapter xxx.

In 1803 the celebrated river we were navigating, though it had all the natural features it possesses to-day, was by no means the same picture of moving life. The steamboats did not appear on its surface until four years later, and the journeys up and down the river were frequently a week in length. In that day the passenger did not hurry on board just as a bell was disturbing the neighborhood, bustling his way through a rude throng of porters, cartmen, orangewomen, and newsboys to save the distance by just a minute and a half, but his luggage was often sent to the vessel the day before; he passed the morning in saying adieu, and when he repaired to the vessel, it was with gentlemanlike leisure, often to pass hours on board previous to sailing; and not infrequently to hear the unwelcome tidings that this event was deferred until the next day. How different, too, was the passage from one in a steamboat. There was no jostling of each other, no scrambling for places at the table, no bolting of food, no impertinence manifested, no swearing about missing the Eastern or Southern boats, or the Schenectady, Saratoga, or Boston trains on account of a screw being loose, nor any other unseemly manifestation that anybody was in a hurry—on the contrary wine and fruit were provided, as if the travellers intended to enjoy themselves, and a journey in that day was a festa. . . . Passages were certainly made in twenty-four hours in the sloops, but these were the exceptions, a week being much more likely to be the time passed in the enjoyment of the beautiful scenery of the river. The vessel usually got aground, once at least, and frequently several times in a trip, and often a day or two were thus delightfully lost giving the stranger an opportunity of visiting the surrounding country. The necessity of anchoring with a foul wind on every opposing tide, too, increased these occasions, thus lending to the excursion something of the character of an exploring expedition. . . . There might have been thirty sail in sight when the *Wallingford* got fairly into the river, some turning down with a young ebb, making fifteen or twenty miles in six hours, and others like ourselves

The Packets

stealing along against it at about the same rate. Half a dozen of these craft were quite near us, and the decks of most of these which were steering north had parties including ladies, evidently proceeding to the "Springs." . . . We were soon coming close up on the quarter of a sloop that had its deck crowded with passengers of the better class, while on the forecastle were several horses and carriages, customary accompaniments to such a scene at that day.

The skipper of the sloop as a rule used a long tiller for steering. The wheel was slow in coming into use. In beating to windward he always gave his boat a good "full" and in going about he liked to forereach. How the loose and heavy canvas of the sloop flapped and roared while she was in stays and what a cloud of lime dust arose from the sails when the first trips of the season were being made! The sloop was "able" and could carry sail in a fresh wind. To shorten sail the taking in of the topsail was generally sufficient and the necessity of reefing was rare. To do this the mainsail was lowered the required space, and fastened securely at the leech and hoist only. Reef points or nettles were not always used, nor were they needed to prevent the loose canvas from bulging out along the boom, for the "lazy jacks" kept that part of the sail in place. As for the jib it seldom had a bonnet, and was carried full with a reefed mainsail, except in thunder squalls, which generally struck the river from the westward. Then the mainsail would be lowered about half way down and a small part of the jib set. This was a slouchy reef to be sure, but it was surprising how well it served its purpose and what good windward work the sloop would make under it.

I well remember the *Illinois*, when she was owned in Newburgh in 1868, and was said to be fifty years old. Old boatmen said she had been a packet sloop in younger days, having been built in Newburgh, but when I first recall her she was carrying lumber between Albany and Newburgh. Many a gay party have I taken part in when

The Packets

this sloop was chartered for a day's excursion on the river, or by moonlight. The broad, clean deck covered by an awning made a capital place for dancing or games. Small boats were carried so that we might go ashore at the many different points of interest along the banks. The *Illinois* was lost off Point Judith. When she was a packet sloop her captain was Elijah, the father of George D. Woolsey, whose reminiscences follow.

The *Illinois* was painted with stripes of somewhat gaudy colors, as was the fashion of the times, but not so elaborately as the Nyack sloops. They were very smart in their appearance and good sailers too, for now and then, as they passed through Newburgh bay on the way up or down the river, they would try conclusions with our home sloops and sometimes worst them. The *Illinois* carried but three sails, mainsail, jib, and topsail. The latter was attached to the topmast by hoops like the mainsail, and sheeted out to the end of the gaff. There was no "club" to it, nor did it set much flatter than the mainsail or jib. It seems to have been the idea of the old time sail-makers that a certain amount of "bag" was an advantage and some of the sailing masters and skippers shared this error. They would occasionally declare that a flat sail did not hold the wind and that it was better to have the leech shortened so as to give the rest of the sail room to belly out a little, and this was quite compatible with their ideas of keeping the sail "rap" full, when beating to windward, and never "pinching."

The result of this was that the old sloops did not point as high as the modern yacht with her flat sails, yet she went through the water at a good pace so that when she went into stays to go about on the other tack she forereached several times her own length, though often losing a good deal of her way in so doing. But as the jib was used to aid in putting the boat on the other tack the older skippers could not be made to see that

The Packets

what they gained to windward in being several minutes in stays was much more than lost in the speed and momentum that the new yacht retains in going on the other tack at once. I shall never forget the reproof that I once got as a boy from an experienced old skipper of New Hamburgh after a race of small sloops and catboats. Said he:

Why the —— did you always put your "helem" over so hard when you went about. I seen you do it over and over agin, and now after all our scrapin', and pot leadin' her bottom, and tightenin' the leech you've lost the race. Why did n't you let her go 'round easy and not slam your rudder over as if it was a barn door on a cold day. Gosh, Willie, I thought you knew better nor that. But you worked the tide right this time, in crossin' the river at Danskammer P'int, and not fightin' the ebb, as most of the others done by huggin' the east shore.

The *Mohican*[1] had been a famous sloop, albeit she fell to carrying limestone from

[1] See List of Vessels; page 94. —. W. E. V.

the quarries at Malden to the blast furnaces that formerly were places of activity along the river for reducing the ores of Dutchess and Orange counties. At Cold Spring, Poughkeepsie, and Peekskill there were several such thirty years ago. To-day they are in ruins, for these industries could not compete with the newer ones of Pennsylvania and the Southern States where the coal and the ores are close together. How brilliantly the sky was illuminated at night on Newburgh bay when the furnace at Kaal Rock[1] Poughkeepsie, or at Cold Spring was opened.

One afternoon I was on the *Samsondale* beating down the river from Poughkeepsie against a south wind. We were light. The captain expected to get a load at Sherman's Dock, Newburgh. As we passed New Hamburgh the *Mohican* was getting under way bound for Fort Montgomery. She was standing toward the Reef buoy, and was

---

[1] From the Dutch word "Kallen." Vessels were formerly hailed here.—W. E. V.

The Packets

soon near us. The wind freshened as we passed the reef, and the "sea" began to get up under the ever-increasing tide and a wind that now had a sweep of nearly ten miles up the bay. The waves were dashing over the deck forward of the mast, and the foot of the jib was wet with spray. This gave the *Mohican* a slight advantage over our boat. It was nip and tuck between us until we got to the middle of Newburgh bay where the wind had become a reefing breeze and the ebb-tide had kicked up a sea that made the ferry-boat roll as she crossed back and forth in the trough. It was then that the *Mohican* began to forge ahead, and she crossed our bow before we put in at Sherman's Dock. We were indeed disgusted and our captain was full of reasons to explain the defeat. I had felt confident that we would win, though realizing that the *Mohican* was a fast boat. Neither of us carried topsails the last hour; they had to be taken in soon after passing Danskammer Point (the Devil's Dance Chamber made famous by Irving). How the topsails ballooned out when they were first lowered to the crosstrees!—and it took some time to clew them down.

The North River sloop when running directly before the wind was at her worst. The jib hung idle and useless, lazily flapping from time to time, for there was no effort made to throw it out opposite the mainsail as is done with the spinnaker of a yacht, and with her long boom well out toward the shrouds it was inevitable that she would steer hard and have a tendency to yaw and luff. Jibing occasionally became necessary, even though the wind held steady. The many reaches of the river run in somewhat different directions so that the captain had to change his mainsail from one side to the other as he sailed up or down stream before the wind. To do this successfully in a fresh wind was a feat requiring no little skill, for the big booms were from seventy-five to ninety feet in length and were they

The Packets

allowed to "fetch up" suddenly the mast would be apt to be carried away. To obviate this danger, the sailing master would put his helm hard up and keep it there until the vessel was at an angle of nearly forty-five degrees to her course, then the big mainsail would take the wind on the other side and begin to swing around dragging the loose mainsheet with it, all the while gaining velocity. For a few moments you think there is going to be a big smash, especially when the boom passes over the taffrail with a roar. But no, for the skipper has kept his helm hard up all the while and the big sloop has turned more and more so that before the mainsheet is taut again, the wind has caught the mainsail on the other side and it is all aluff. The helm is then thrown to the opposite side, the jib hauled to windward, and the sloop is on her course again.

The schooner has a decided advantage in running before the wind, for then the foresail is thrown out opposite the mainsail wing and wing and jibing is not so difficult; but when it becomes necessary, the peak of the mainsail has to be lowered when the wind is fresh, for the tactics of jibing a sloop cannot be followed. The two-master began to be a favorite rig on the river in the late sixties. In some instances sloops were altered into schooners. The old sloop *Milan* of Rondout, for instance, had capsized off Cornwall in a fresh southeaster when carrying a cargo of flagstone, and was afterwards raised and appeared as a schooner under the name of *George Hurst*.

The North River schooner differed greatly from the "Down East" schooner that formerly sailed up the river for coal as far as Newburgh, or Rondout where the Delaware and Hudson canal reached the river. These vessels, especially when light, were clumsy looking craft with their blunt bows and bowsprits pointed high. How sluggish they were compared with the North River vessels. We used to say of them that they were built by the mile and sawn off to suit,

The Packets 35

so devoid of lines or models were they. Yet these "Down Easters" could sail well when in their element. The North River schooner was built on somewhat the same plan as the sloop, having a centre board, and her bowsprit carried out almost horizontal, and one head-sail, the single jib, attached to a jib-boom, as with the sloop.[1] She carried no foretopmast. The skippers contented themselves with a maintopsail only and set it like the sloop's. The foresail was of good size compared with the mainsail and not a mere "ribbon" such as the racing schooner yacht now carries. The quarter-deck was replaced in the later schooners by a trunk cabin, lighted from the side and end, affording smaller and less pleasant accommodations than those below the quarter-decks of the old packet sloops with their large windows for light and air at the stern.

The Greene County Tanner was a good example of an old North River schooner.

---

[1] A few of the later schooners carried a flying-jib.— W. E. V.

She was built at Catskill in 1832 and had been a sloop in her earlier days. I well remember her as she passed through Newburgh bay or at other points along the river on her frequent trips, carrying different sorts of cargoes, for as time went on her owners became less particular as to what was put aboard of her. She was often engaged in the flagstone trade—large quantities of the stone being quarried in Ulster and Greene counties. The latter county gave the boat her name and freights, for it was the home of the industry of tanning hides with the bark of hemlock and so energetically was it carried on that the trees are well-nigh exterminated.

It was the morning after the assassination of President Lincoln when I first recollect this schooner. I was in a rowboat with my father who was rowing to Newburgh from our place on the opposite shore about three miles north. It was Saturday and there was no school. The wind was from the south and the tide on the last of the ebb,

The Packets

as we reached the channel. Being a mere lad I was set at steering, and felt very important when I reported a schooner approaching. Her mainsheet was dragging in the water so light was the wind, and jib and foresail stood flat and lifeless. We passed close under her stern and I read her name as the sailing master shouted to us the news of the appalling tragedy at Washington on the night before. I can see the schooner now as she swung slowly around when the skipper left the wheel and ran to the end of the taffrail to tell us all that he knew of the details of the murder.

The schooners were not as good in windward work as the sloop, but with a fair or beam wind they were faster. The rig, however, soon commended itself, for the sloop with her long boom, tall mast, and heavy mainsail was difficult to handle at all times and especially in a blow and required a crew of six men to the schooner's four. The first of the schooners were converted sloops, from which many of the larger ones were changed to save expense of operation. Later, about 1865 there was built a new type of schooner for the Hudson which though rigged the same was a wider and shallower boat thus giving her greater carrying capacity and permitting all the cargo to be placed on deck for expedition in loading and unloading. She was quite sharp forward, which—with other good points in her model—made her a good sailer. Of this type was the *Robert A. Forsythe* of Newburgh, between which place and Albany she plied as a carrier of lumber. The *Wm. A. Ripley* of Low Point on Newburgh bay was another schooner of somewhat the same style and rig. The *Ripley* was built at Newark, N. J., in 1874 and was sixty-nine feet in length and twenty-two feet beam. Her carrying capacity was one hundred and twenty-five tons. Her captain was Robert S. Collyer.[1]

The packets had virtually disappeared

---

[1] The *Uriah F. Washburn*, built by Jacob Woolsey at Tompkins Cove in 1866, was undoubtedly the best ex-

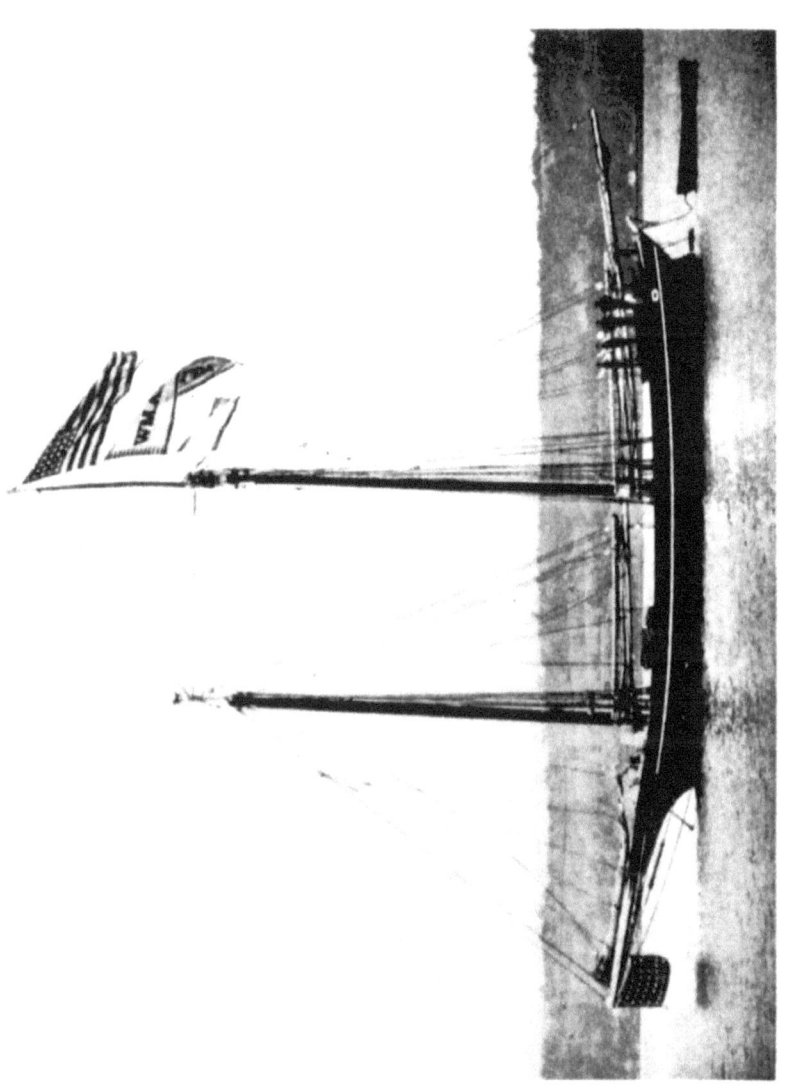

SCHOONER "WM. A. RIPLEY," FORMERLY OWNED BY ROBERT COLLYER OF CHELSEA

From an old photograph

The Packets

when the schooner began to be a favorite rig, and none of them so far as I know ever ran as a packet boat for passengers.

The sloop in the early days was a seagoer, making voyages to the West Indies; even the North River and Sound sloops ventured so far amain. A sea-going sloop of my early boyhood that joined the company of North River vessels was the old *Benjamin Franklin*. She had been built in Huntington, Long Island, in 1836 for the trade between New Bedford and the West Indies, taking out cattle and fetching molasses back. Her length was sixty-five feet and her beam twenty-one and her capacity eighty-five tons; a small vessel for such a trade we would account her to-day. She was owned at one time by John Van

---

ample of these modern schooners. Her captain was James Monahan, who sailed her for 17 years, and is now first pilot of the steamer *City of Newburgh* of the Central Hudson Steamboat Co. This schooner was built for the Washburn Bros., brick-makers of Glasco-on-Hudson, and she now hails from Perth Amboy, N. J. Her carrying capacity was about 200 tons.—W. E. V.

Keuren of Poughkeepsie, who sold her in 1864 to the late John L. Collyer while he was living at Tivoli, then known as Upper Red Hook. But afterwards her owner moved to Low Point, now Chelsea, on Newburgh bay. Although much like other sloops of the time, she had some features that were different. There was more free-board and her bow was blunter. In her younger days she had carried a large topsail but when I knew her she contented herself with only two sails. In fact the sloops began to dispense with topsails when wages got high after the Civil War, for they were difficult to handle and required an extra man. But the *Benjamin Franklin* was a fast sailer and under her lessened canvas, when the wind blew fresh from the south and the ebb-tide had kicked up a sea, it was then that she was in her element and could show the way to many of the fast sloops of the river.[1]

[1] The flood-tide and northeast wind make a greater sea on the Newburgh bay.—W. E. V.

The Packets

J. L. Collyer had previously owned and sailed the *First Effort*, a packet sloop sailing between Red Hook and New York, and later he owned the sloop *Perseverance*. This was before the Hudson River railroad was built when the only other means of communication along the river was the stage-coach over the Albany post-road, a slow and uncomfortable journey. J. L. Collyer was a brother of the late Thomas Collyer who in his younger days was a sloop builder and afterwards with Daniel Drew built the Hudson River steamboats *Daniel Drew*, *Armenia*, and others.

When the steamboat began to take passengers away from the packet sloops they became in turn "market boats." Their business consisted of taking on produce at points along the river and selling it on arrival at New York, carrying back drygoods, etc. Such a trip from say Catskill or Kingston was completed in ten to twelve days,—Captain John L. Collyer maintained such a line from Tivoli for several years.

This business was in turn absorbed by large double deck barges towed by steamboats. The barges were fitted with sleeping accommodations, and many trips have I made on them. The bleating of the calves and sheep from the lower regions of the boat was not conducive to sleep. Many of these barges still survive here and there along the upper river. The propellers and side-wheelers of the Hudson River companies now control this large and lucrative business.

The Middle Grounds of the Upper Hudson were a vexation to the early navigators, and they still perplex the inexperienced, albeit they are now marked with lights, buoys, black and red. These sunken shoals conceal no rocks. Did they do so the "bones" of many vessels would now be found on them. These shoals are flats of mud and sand, and at high tide are covered by three to four feet of water, enough to conceal the sedge grass or water weeds that grow there, and which, at low water, are plainly seen

The Packets

only when full grown at midsummer. How easy it was to run on them, there to lie with your keel in the soft mud until the tide fell and rose again, unless perchance you went on at low water. But more likely it would be at high water while running up the river before a strong southerly wind. Before it was possible to change your course your boat was in shoal water and refused to answer her helm and soon you were hard aground.

Vessels have been known to go on so hard and fast that they had to be dug off, even after removing the cargo. A schooner from Long Island went on the Middle Grounds in the Livingston channel just above Tivoli about forty years ago and lay there nearly a month, and was finally released at great expense. But it was seldom that the sloops were caught in this way, so familiar were their skippers with the river, its shoals, reefs, and tides. The Middle Grounds are in the upper Hudson where the water is always fresh. They begin a short distance south of Kingston Point near the Esopus lighthouse, and extend all the way to Albany in perplexing irregularity. Between Catskill and Coxsackie there are several baffling ones. Formerly there were two channels between Hudson and Albany with a chain of islands and Middle Grounds occupying the centre of the river. They are shown on an old map which I have, made in 1810, and which is called "Hudson's River from Sandy Hook to Sandy Hill"—a point north of Saratoga where the river turns sharply to the west. The dredging and diking operations of the Federal Government have since resulted in a single and well marked channel below Albany.

There was formerly a picturesque sight which was occasionally seen before the passing of the sail from the Hudson. This was the fleet of sloops and schooners, twenty-five to thirty in number, which the prevalence of heavy westerly winds brought together at the south end of the Highlands.

The Packets 45

With such winds vessels leaving New York and bound up the river would reach Jones Point off the Dunderberg to find it impossible to pass through the Race.[1] Here the river's turn to the westward would cause the wind to be dead ahead, and as the flood-tides had been so weakened by the prevalence of such winds, it would not be possible for the vessels to proceed farther and thus they assembled as they came up from below.

It was near this point that Captain Kidd's treasure ship was supposed to have sunk and for years fruitless efforts were made to find her. Old boatmen have told me that as many as fifty vessels would be wind-

---

[1] The Race extends from the southeastern end of the Dunderberg to Anthony's Nose in the Highlands. Washington Irving jocosely accounts for the name by saying that one morning as the sun rose over the mountains its rays glanced from the rubicund nose of the redoubtable Anthony Van Corlears who was on the deck of a sloop on a voyage to Fort Orange, and killed a sturgeon that was swimming near the surface. The fame of this event was so great that the promontory was ever afterwards known as Anthony's Nose.—W.E.V.

bound here. When the southerly wind came at last or the flood-tide reasserted itself the boats all started, slowly growing apart as the faster ones began to draw away from the others. Still it would take an hour or more before the fleet was disbanded. By the time Newburgh bay, twenty miles above, was reached the vessels would be strung out into a line a mile or more long.

Among the sloops of Fishkill on Newburgh bay were the *Commodore Jones*, and the *New Jersey*, which were owned by the late Thomas Aldridge, who had extensive brickyards at Dutchess Junction. The captain of the *Jones* was John Paye of Fishkill. He is now a brick manufacturer, for he retired from boating long since, but is fond of relating his experiences on the river in past days. He began sailing the river before he was twenty, and became the skipper of the *Commodore Jones* over fifty years ago. She was the fastest sloop above the Highlands and has made the

The Packets

record for the round trip to New York and return from Fishkill. She was built at Derby, Conn., in 1835. Her companion sloop the *New Jersey* was built in 1830. Other sailing vessels of Fishkill were the sloop *Delaware*, of which Larrie Flarrety was captain, and the schooner *Thomas Jefferson*, afterwards called the *Carrie McLean*. The *Commodore Jones*, like other sloops and schooners of the Hudson, was registered at the U. S. Custom House in New York. Her capacity was one hundred tons, though the registered tonnage was considerably less. Captain Paye assures me that he once made the run from New York to Denning's Point (on Newburgh bay), fifty-eight miles up, in four and one half hours with the schooner *Harriet Ann*. Once, in 1868, he left Hamilton Ferry, Brooklyn, with the sloop *Commodore Jones* at nine P. M., wind east-northeast, went to Fishkill, and was back at Hamilton Ferry at eight P.M. next day. Of the twenty-three hours' interval, four were spent in loading.

The usual time required for a sloop or a schooner to beat down to New York from Fishkill or Newburgh was "two ebbs" and "one flood" as the boatmen put it. The vessels would get underway at high water, when they could pass off the Flats fully loaded, thence with the favoring ebb they passed down through the Highlands, and Verplanck's Point was reached in about five hours. The flood-tide would now be encountered, but even though the wind was light good headway could be made against it by keeping on the Croton Flats with the centreboard half down. Thence they passed into Tappan Zee and over on to the Nyack Flats to avoid the strength of the flood. By the time Piermont was reached the ebb-tide had again begun to make, and with it New York was reached in about five hours more. In other words the trip from Fishkill against the wind was made in fifteen or sixteen hours. With wind abeam or fair, the run was made in half the time. The sloops always sailed at night

The Packets

unless wind or tide was unfavorable. During periods of calm, there were occasionally "land" breezes at night, that is, currents of air that drew strongly from the shore toward the river. Off the Palisades or the "Rocks" as the boatmen called them, there is at times a decided land breeze of this sort which was always observed and taken advantage of by the skippers. While it had been quite calm all over the river through the day and early part of the night during the summer months, in the "small hours" these breezes would rise and carry a vessel for several miles.

The flood-tides in the Lower Hudson, so the boatmen declare, have tricks that are hard to account for. They will tell you that the tide sometimes rises while the current is running down on the surface, and that a deeply laden vessel will feel the influence of the current moving up while the light vessel is held back by the surface current moving in the opposite direction, and this they declare is not dependent upon the wind. The moon's position with relation to the earth has of course a marked effect upon the tide as is well known. Thus the tides are apt to run low when the moon is in Apogee, "Pogy Tides" as they are called in New England, while when the moon is near the earth or in Perigee the tides are apt to run higher. On Newburgh bay I have heard the boatmen speak of these moons as "Pear Tree" and "Apple Tree" moons, and of "Witch Tides." By this they meant a slow flood. Now and then along the river when progress was slow and there were three or four days of calm weather, on a still night when not more than four or five miles would be made on one tide, and the vessels would drift together, and oftentimes foul each other, particularly in the Highlands, the conversation between the captains would be like this:

Captain of *Benj. Franklin*—"Well, this is very slow, getting up. I have only drifted ten miles in the last two tides (twenty-four hours)."

THE PALISADES OF THE HUDSON

From a photograph by W. J. Wilson

The Packets

Captain of *Sam'l Marsh* [1]—"Yes, Captain John, we are having 'Witch Tides.' The moon is in the 'Apple Tree' and tides is running poor. No floods. No wind."

Captain of *Benj. Franklin*—"I guess to-morrow the flood will bring a good breeze of south wind. I see the cobwebs hanging in the rigging."

Captain of *Sam'l Marsh*—"I hope so. I have been three days getting up from New York to the Highlands."

And the next day a good south wind would come.

The old sloops were formerly furnished with long oars known as "sweeps" which were used, particularly in the Highlands, during calms to to prevent the vessels being run ashore by the tide, for the currents there are swift and at certain places would throw a sloop on the rocks were she not kept off. But in later years the sweeps were done away with and the yawl boat used to keep the sloop on her course by towing when the wind failed.

[1] Her captain was John Ward of Cornwall, a brother of the champion oarsmen.—W. E. V.

The upper end of the Highlands from Cold Spring to Storm King[1] is called the "Worragut," a corruption, perhaps, of the old Dutch name. On this reach, especially when the wind is westerly in the spring and fall of the year, there is apt to be a gale which draws down from Pollopel Island past Crow's Nest to Little Stony Point. The wind at this point is directly down the river and sometimes attains a high velocity, so much so that the sloops and schooners often have to run under bare poles, with all sails lashed down. In 1824 the packet sloop *Neptune* of Newburgh was capsized here by a flaw while beating up the river and thirty-five passengers were drowned.

Owing to the tide being earlier in the

[1] Formerly Butter Hill with Breakneck on the opposite bank. The name was changed at the instance of the late N. P. Willis, whose country seat, Idlewild, was at its base near Moodna Creek, formerly Murderer's Creek, a change also made at Mr. Willis's suggestion. Newburgh bay begins at this point and extends northward to beyond Danskammer Point, a distance of about 12 miles. On this reach the river has a width of over a mile.—W. E. V.

CAPTAIN JOHN PAYE OF FISHKILL
From a photograph by Cramer, Matteawan, N. Y.

The Packets

East River than the North, a sailing vessel can run down the East River on the first of the ebb, round the Battery and find the flood still running in the North; or she can go down the North River on the last of the ebb round the Battery and take the flood-tide which will then be running in the East River.

A sailing master of long experience furnishes this information:

Down river with head winds—With a good full-sail breeze of head wind from Catskill to New York it would take the average vessel, sloop or schooner about five ebb-tides to beat down. Up river with head winds—I have come around the Battery several times about six P.M. at nearly high slack water with the wind northwest by west (which is one of the best head winds to beat up the river with). Beat a full ebb-tide out, took the first of the flood about Piermont and went to Low Point on that tide. That would be called beating from New York to Low Point in one flood tide.

This captain added that the longest time

Sloops of the Hudson

he ever took to reach the upper end of Newburgh bay from New York was five days which was due to being wind bound at the south end of the Highlands.[1] One of the shortest round trips was that of the *Henrietta Collyer*.[2] She was a schooner built in Nyack in 1880, for the iron trade which was then carried on along the river, and in which about a dozen sailing vessels were profitably engaged, carrying iron ore and limestone to the blast furnaces and taking away the pig iron,—a business that has now all ceased as I have mentioned. This schooner left the Manhattan Iron Works, which was then (1880) at 140th Street and North River, at six P.M., with a fresh south wind and flood-tide. At eight o'clock the next morning she was at Catskill one hundred and fifteen miles up the river. She went up light. By noon that day the schooner was loaded with limestone and got under way with a northwest wind, and at three o'clock

---

[1] Calms and poor floods produced the same.—W. E. V.
[2] Her captain was M. W. Collyer.—W. E. V.

The Packets 55

the next morning she was back at the dock of the Iron Works.

During the Civil War, and for a few years after, canvas became very dear, and the sloop owners were reluctant to fit with new sails when needed, and often when the wind was fresh several sloops and schooners would be seen lying at anchor rather than risk having their old sails blown away while beating to windward.

In 1860 there were as many as two hundred sloops and schooners engaged in the commerce of the Hudson, some of which had been built as early as 1816 such as the sloop *Mad Anthony* now of Verplanck's Point. She is still in commission, and is the oldest sailing vessel afloat on the river to-day.[1] The records of the Custom House at New York contain the names of many of these vessels though it is hard to identify them owing to change of names. The largest sloop on the river was the *Utica* of Athens,—

[1] She was altered into a schooner several years ago.
—W. E. V.

two hundred and twenty tons' capacity, built at Albany in 1833. She was sailing as late as 1890, but is now a lighter in New York Harbor. Other up-river sloops of the seventies were the sloop *Bolivar* of New Baltimore, built in 1826, and the *Victory* of Athens, built in 1814. She had no centreboard, being a keel vessel like the *Illinois* of Newburgh.

Capt. N. S. Cooper, who is now Superintendent of the Catskill and Hudson Steamboat Company and until recently captain of the steamer *Onteora*, comes of an old family of North River sloop owners. With his father, Ira Cooper of Athens, he owned and sailed various sloops, among others the *Dutchess*, *Victory*, *Utica*, *Holbrook*, and *Reindeer*. Captain Cooper has kindly contributed the following information:

In the year 1864, the *Sally Frances* was sunk at Red Hook, Brooklyn, in a blow.

September 30, 1876, the schooner *Dutchess* was sunk at Barrytown Bluff, by the steamer *St. John*.

The Packets

October, 17, 1879, the schooner *Catskill* was sunk by the steamer *City of Troy*, off the plaster mills at Newburgh.

August 15, 1888, the *Holbrook* was sunk by the *Saratoga* off Catskill Point.

April 12, 1889, the *Revenue* was sunk by the Peoples' Line steamer *Drew* at Esopus.

The *Victory* was sold to a party in Brooklyn by the name of Hall, who changed her into a lighter. The *Reindeer* was also sold to the same party.

The sloop *Congress* was put on the beach in Rondout Creek, near the West Shore R. R. Bridge.

A veteran captain of the upper Hudson was Capt. A. Wesley Hale. Not long before his death, July, 1906, he published, in the Saugerties *Herald*, part of his recollections of the river. The following is quoted from that newspaper:

I saw a short time ago a statement in your paper written by a Newburgh friend and I think he is laboring under a false impression when he says our big single stick sloops were unmanageable unless under full sail, or as he expresses it, under a full spread of canvas. Some of our big sloops, such as the *Tanner* was when a sloop, and the *Utica*, the *Oregon*, the *Canaan*, the *Wm. Mayo*, the *Asa Bigelow*, the *Gideon Lee*, and hundreds of others that I could mention would go to windward or any other way under a two reef, and many of them under a three reef sail and turn around, or go about as the boatmen say, almost as quick as our ice boats. And then he says the *Tanner* had a mast one hundred and six feet and topmast fifty-eight feet, and she hailed from Saugerties, eight miles above Kingston. Saugerties is twelve miles above Kingston, and the *Tanner* never hailed from Saugerties, and never had a long topmast when a sloop; her mast was ninety-six feet only with a short topmast. She carried a large square topsail, and only used it when sailing with a fair wind. The *Tanner* was built at Catskill in 1832, and hailed from Catskill until bought by the well known Captain called Gus (Augustus) Decker, to run from Wilbur carrying wood and stone to New York. He afterwards sold her to Ezra Fitch to run in the stone and lumber trade. In about the year 1850 she lay up at Rondout. There

CAPTAIN AUGUSTUS WESLEY HALE LATE OF SAUGERTIES
From a photograph by Austin

was a fire that winter near where she laid up. The sparks set her rigging on fire and her rigging and spar were burned to her deck. She was then rigged into a schooner and had a long topmast and jib-boom. Capt. Wm. Hyde then bought an interest in her and sailed her nearly forty years, carrying stone from Wilbur to Eastern ports. She carried her mainmast away in a blow near Point Judith, and lost mast, rigging, and mainsail. A fishing smack found it and towed it to Newport. The *Tanner* is still in the stone trade.

The *Wm. Mayo* was built at Coxsackie in 1836 by Wm. Mayo and she has quite a record. She was bought by Robt. Kerr to carry stone from Wilbur. Capt. James Schoonmaker took command of her. He capsized her and carried her topmast away. In about 1846, E. J. McCarthy bought her to carry stone from Saugerties. She changed captains quite frequently. Capts. Josiah Joy, David Searles, Chas. Felto, Harry Snyder, Andrew Simmons, and others commanded her. Capt. Joy capsized her in a squall opposite Poughkeepsie and her mast landed on the ferryboat's deck. Capt. David Searles in a race from New London to Newport against the smart sloop, *Oliver Ames,* when near Point Judith, carried her mast away. The *Ames,* after three trials, succeeded in getting a hawser to her, and towed her into Newport, costing the owner, J. P. Russell, over $500.

In 1868 J. P. Russell rebuilt the *Mayo* at an expense of $12,000. He then rigged her into a schooner, and J. V. L. Crum took charge of her. A few years after, Capt. Crum, when bound to Newark, struck rock and sunk her near Shooter's Island in quite shoal water. They got her up, and about 1874 J. P. Russell sold her to John Maxwell. Ezra Whitaker then took charge of her and ran her to Eastern ports with stone.

In 1879, while laying at anchor in Flushing bay in a northeast gale, she dragged her anchors and went ashore on the rocks on Riker's Island and filled with water. In 1880, when bound down the East River loaded with sand for the rubbing mill at Malden, he made a mistake and ran her in a slip near Bridge Street, E. R., striking a ship, and carried both masts away. He tore the sails into ribbons and smashed a barge's stern all in, and came very near sinking her. After that they ran her as a barge until 1882, when she was sold to New Jersey

The Packets

parties, and she is now a lighter in New York harbor.

The *Oregon* was built at Coxsackie in 1846 for parties in Coeymans. Her mast was ninety-four feet long and twenty-eight inches in the partners. It came from the West, I think from Oregon, and cost $500. Her topmast was sixty-five feet. The *Oregon* was one of the first North River sloops that carried a long topmast and gaff topsail. About the year 1850 Wm. F. Russell bought her from Coeymans to carry iron from the Ulster iron mill. Capt. Peter Sickles took command of her. In 1867 Capt. Jeremiah Paris bought her. He ran her in the stone trade a short time, and then rigged her into a schooner and ran her to the East with stone and lumber.

The sloop *Canaan* was built at Albany in 1826. Capt. Levi Freligh bought her in 1851. In 1853 he transferred half of her to his son, Capt. B. M. Freligh. B. M. was captain. His brother Peter was sailing master, and Austin was captain of the forecastle. She was a hard weather sloop. She was called the old horse, and very few, if any, could blanket her when beating up the river in a heavy northeast blow.

Capt. Freligh ran her principally in the brick trade. At one time brick was dull, he took a load of lumber from Albany to Providence, R. I. When going around Point Judith they got caught in a blow and had a rough time. They were all fresh-water sailors, and they thought their time had come, but being a good able vessel, she weathered the gale, and they reached Providence all right. They did not make another trip.

The sloop *Victory* was built at Marlborough, N. Y., in 1814. She ran as a merchant sloop and carried passengers for several years, and was afterwards bought by John V. L. Overbaugh and Wm. Thorp to carry brick from Glasco. In about 1843 they rebuilt her and raised her main deck. In about 1868 they sold her to Capt. Ira Cooper of Athens. He again rebuilt her and made her a flush deck. About 1890 he sold her to New York parties, and she is now a lighter in New York harbor.

The *Bucktail*, afterwards converted into a schooner and called the *Dutchess*, the *Catskill* a schooner which sank in Newburgh bay, and the big sloops *Addison* and *Am-*

The Packets

bassador, built at Coxsackie in 1819, and the *Iowa* of Malden, were among the other up-river vessels of my time. Poughkeepsie was the home port of several more. The two blast furnaces, the famous Buckeye mowing-machine works, the Vassar brewery, and other industries gave them profitable freights. In earlier days Poughkeepsie had even sent out whaling vessels and the Whale Dock is still pointed out. The *Mohican* was one of the old sloops that hailed from this port. She was built in 1837 at Peekskill by Isaac Depew, Senator Depew's father, who ran her as a packet and market boat. During the Civil War she passed into the possession of Edward Tower and others who were interested in the furnaces and who used her in conveying limestone and iron ore to the Tower furnaces at Poughkeepsie. Her skipper was Joseph Reynolds. The *Mohican* was sixty-eight feet long, twenty-five feet beam. Under her quarterdeck, which extended almost to midships, were a dozen berths. She was always painted red, and was a fast sailer. Her timbers and planking were of locust and white oak. The old sloop now lies on the shore at Chelsea in front of the home of Captain Moses W. Collyer who brought her there for a breakwater and dock a few years ago when she was dismantled and withdrawn from the river. Other vessels of Poughkeepsie were the big sloop *Margaret*, built at Sing Sing in 1835 (her captain was Abe Lansing), the schooners *Buckeye*, *Flying Cloud*, and *Peter Valleau*, pronounced by the boatmen "Vallew." The last two plied between Newburgh and Poughkeepsie, while the *Margaret* brought lumber from Albany. The *Henry Barclay*, the *Kemble*, and the *Annie Tower* like the *Mohican* were employed in the iron trade.

At New Hamburgh eight miles below there were, among other boats, the sloops *Mary Dallas* and *General Ward*, and the scow sloop *Little Martha* of which "Clint" Williams was skipper. He and his two brothers,

The Packets 65

colored men, comprised the crew, and capital boatmen they were.

The Leroy brothers, William, Peter, and Charles, as well as the Drake brothers, Charles, William, and Martin, were all experienced and skilful boatmen. They could also handle small yachts with great ability. For both William Drake's and Peter Leroy's skill in this respect I had great admiration. They, too, were experts in handling ice-boats, and when Peter Leroy had the tiller of the *Zero*, there were few yachts on the ice between Poughkeepsie or Newburgh that could pass him.[1] William and Peter Leroy were excellent shots, and no one knew better than they where to find woodcock and quail. The Leroys were among the first to foresee the doom of the sloop, and about 1876 they built the first

[1] Other ice-boats of this neighborhood were the *Flying Cloud*, owned by Mr. Irving Grinnell, and the giant *Icicle*, by Mr. John E. Roosevelt; but the latter was so heavy that she showed her speed only in a heavy wind and on hard ice. On Capt. M. W. Collyer's *Vision* I have run from Newburgh to Danskammer Point, a distance of six miles, in seven minutes.—W. E. V.

66   Sloops of the Hudson

of the barges for Garner & Co. This was the *Mary and Emma*—a vessel of about three hundred tons' carrying capacity.

Captain Martin Drake has kindly contributed the following:

I will give you as near as I can, the vessels and their captains, belonging to New Hamburgh, from about 1860 to 1873 or 1875:

	NAME	CAPTAIN
Sloop	*John I. Wiltse*	Charles S. Drake
"	*Utica* [1]	Charles S. Drake
"	*Ella Jane*	William Percival
"	*David Sands*	Jacob Leroy
"	*General Ward*	William P. Drake
"	*James Coats*	James R. Lawson
"	*Harriet Martha*	Charles Leroy
"	*Mary Dallas*	Martin V. Drake
"	*North America*	Austin Griffin
"	*Samuel Cunningham*	William P. Drake
"	*Revenue*	Charles S. Drake
"	*Reputation*	Van Nort Carpenter
"	*Joseph Griggs*	Marvin Vananden
"	*Lucy Hopkins*	Martin Griffin
"	*Victory*	Charles Leroy
"	*Jane Grant*	William P. Drake

[1] Largest sloop on the river, as already mentioned, but she was not fast, though a good sailer.—W. E. V.

CAPTAIN MARTIN V. DRAKE OF NEW HAMBURGH
From a photograph by the Benedict Studios, New York

The Packets

	NAME	CAPTAIN
Sloop	Abraham Jones	William B. Leroy
"	First Effort	Peter Leroy
"	Little Martha	Clinton Williams
"	Kate Hale	Charles S. Drake
"	Pennsylvania	William P. Drake
"	Exchange	William P. Drake
"	Samuel Hall	Harry Smith
Schooner	Prize	Austin Griffin
"	Celeste	Martin V. Drake
"	Chas. Rockwood	Edward Griffin
"	Glaucus	Charles S. Drake
"	Anna	William P. Drake
"	Missouri	Harry Smith
"	Christopher Columbus	Charles S. Drake

The only captains living now are Charles Leroy, Austin Griffin, Clinton Williams, William P. Drake, and myself.

Will mention a few incidents:

The sloop *General Ward's* bones lie at Croton on the Hudson, and those of the sloop *Climax* are at New Windsor, and of the sloop *North America*, at Hampton.

The sloop *James Coats* was rounding West Point, when the main sheet caught around the neck of Benj. Hunt, and severed his head from his body, the head going overboard leaving the body on deck. This happened in the summer of 1866.

Sloop *Mary Dallas* capsized on Long Island Sound, E. S. E. of Faulkner's Island, and was towed into New London by the tug *Wellington*, August 6, 1866.

Sloop *David Sands* was sunk in collision with a steamer New York harbor, and three out of five of the crew were drowned.

Sloops *General Ward* and *James Coats* came near being burned in the great railroad accident at New Hamburgh drawbridge where Doc. Simmons, engineer, and twenty-three passengers lost their lives, February 6, 1871.

At Low Point (now Chelsea) they could boast of eight sloops and schooners during the period between 1868 and 1888. In the list were the *Benjamin Franklin, Lydia White, Iron Age, Fancy, Wm. A. Ripley*, and *Henrietta Collyer*. During this period Newburgh was the home port of nearly twenty sailing vessels. In this list were the *Illinois*, of which "Pomp" (James) Wilson was captain, and the *Samsondale*,

SLOOP "MARY DALLAS,"
OWNED BY CAPTAIN MARTIN V. DRAKE OF NEW HAMBURGH

From an oil painting owned by him

The Packets 69

whose captain was George Woolsey. He had a good voice and was fond of singing as he stood on the quarter-deck by the tiller of a moonlight night. In Part III. will be found the reminiscences of Captain Woolsey, which his widow has kindly given for publication.

The *Illinois* was wrecked off Point Judith about fifteen years ago. The fate of the *Samsondale* was to become a lighter, and to lay her bones on the Jersey Flats.

Counting the sloops at Cornwall, Fishkill, Low Point, New Hamburgh, and New Windsor with those at Newburgh there were at least thirty sailing vessels hailing from Newburgh bay.

Cold Spring is in the Highlands at the south end of the Worragut, so dreaded by the old Dutch skippers, if Washington Irving is to be believed. This reach has always borne a bad reputation for its baffling and gusty winds. Nevertheless several sloops made that their home port, drawn thither by the blast furnace and the West

Point foundry where the famous Parrott guns were made during the Civil War. Many of them were carried on the *Victorine* of which "Dave" Lyons was captain, who I believe is still living. She was the fastest sloop on the river and once took part in a yacht race at New York and acquitted herself with credit. She kept the river as late as 1890. The sloop was built in 1848 at Piermont, and had a carrying capacity of one hundred and twenty-five tons. She is now a lighter of an Oil Company at Edgewater, N. J. Her companion was the schooner *Norma* built in Nyack in 1852. In the cove between Constitution Island and Cold Spring the old *Missouri* and *John Jones* lie abandoned.

Nyack and Piermont on Tappan Zee were the homes of many sloops and schooners of past days whose sails whitened the waters as they sailed by Point No Point, Verdrietege Hook, and Teller's Point.

It was not until about the year 1862 that sailing vessels on the Hudson were

The Packets

required by law to carry lights at night.[1] Notwithstanding this there were comparatively few collisions, either with each other or with the many fast passenger steamboats that then plied up and down the river. Yet there were noteworthy disasters due to collisions among which were the following:

The schooner *Catskill* while beating down the river the night of October 17, 1879, was struck by the steamboat *Saratoga* off Newburgh, and sunk. She now lies near the track of the ferry at Fishkill, about five hundred feet from the Newburgh shore. On the ebb-tide the ripple of the water running over the hulk can readily be discerned, and serves as a mark for the pilots of the ferry-boat during a fog. In the summer of 1849 the schooner *Noah Brown* collided with the steamer *Empire* in Newburgh bay. The steamer sank and thirty

---

[1] General B. F. Butler, at one time owner of the yacht *America*, was the author of this law as I am credibly informed.—W. E. V.

passengers were drowned. She had just left the dock at Newburgh at the time of collision. The *Empire* was raised and four years later was in collision with the sloop *Chancellor Livingston*. On this occasion the sloop was beating up the river on the night of July 16, 1853. When off New Hamburgh she struck the *Empire* bound from Troy to New York. The impact of the sloop not only threw the steamer's boiler from its bed, but sunk her as well, with the result that many passengers lost their lives from scalding or drowning. The sloop *First Effort*, of which the late John L. Collyer was then owner and captain, was passing at the time and went alongside and rescued many of the passengers. The *Empire* was beached on the east shore a short distance below New Hamburgh.

On the night of the 21st of November, 18—, the sloop *W. W. Reynolds* was beating down the river and off Blue Point—which is about two miles south of Poughkeepsie, where the sloop belonged — she ran into the

The Packets

steamer *Francis Skiddy*. The sloop's bowsprit struck the boiler causing it to explode. Three firemen and several passengers were scalded to death. The steamboat was on her way down the river from Albany to New York, and was then making the return trips by day. She was the only boat that ever made such regular trips. The *Francis Skiddy* was built by George Collyer.

The dangers of jibing, to which reference has already been made, were shockingly exemplified in the case of the sloop *James Coats*, of which James R. Lawson was captain. This sloop ran between Kingston Point and Brooklyn, and once made the round trip within forty-eight hours. On one occasion in the year 1865, or '66, she was running down the river with a fair wind and had of course to jibe as she rounded West Point. As the main sheet, all slack, came over the deck it formed a loop over the head of Ben Hunt, who was at the wheel, taking off his head, which fell overboard, leaving the headless trunk lying on the deck. Jibing poles which some sloops carried might have obviated such a casualty.

The sail has almost disappeared from the Hudson, for the big seagoing schooner of three, four, and even five masts that still comes up the river, rarely spreads her sails. She makes part of a great tow— consisting of fifty or sixty vessels that move slowly along the river, drawn by three or four powerful tugs, which in turn have superseded the paddle-wheel towboats of my boyhood. Then the towing steamer was generally an old passenger boat which had had her day on the line between New York and Albany. Stripped of cabins, saloons, and upper deck, a mere skeleton of a boat, she would be seen wearily drawing a huge assemblage of barges, scows, canal boats, and down-east schooners laden with lumber, flagstones, grain, coal, and other commodities. To this extremity had the swift and once popular *Alida* sunk, and she was a melancholy sight indeed, when her

The Packets

former grandeur and the fame of her quick passage between New York and Poughkeepsie, were recalled, which I believe has never been lowered by any of her successors.

Though occasionally a schooner is seen sailing on the river, the North River sloop has vanished from the Hudson.

PART II

THE SAIL IN COMPETITION WITH STEAM[1]

THIS part is a compilation of my experiences and recollections of what I have seen and heard as cabin-boy, master, and owner of Hudson River sloops, schooners, and steam vessels, embracing a period of nearly half a century; beginning in the sixties, first as cabin-boy, then cook, after that, cook and hand before the mast, then as mate, and finally as captain, master, and owner. It is also a record of old North River sloops and schooners, their names, some of their captains, owners, and builders; the trade they were in, and their home ports.

These vessels have all passed away, as well as most of their masters and owners and builders. There is no work for this class of vessel to-day on the Hudson, where

[1] Written by Moses W. Collyer.

CAPTAIN MOSES WAKEMAN COLLYER OF CHELSEA
From a photograph by Whitney, Poughkeepsie, N. Y.

Sail vs. Steam

in my younger days there were hundreds owned and employed.

I was born on the banks of the Hudson River in the town of Red Hook. My father, John L. Collyer, was known in the thirties as a North River sloop boatman, having run from upper Red Hook Landing, now called Tivoli, to New York, as captain and owner of a North River packet sloop, which was engaged in carrying farmers' produce and passengers to New York, and general merchandise on his return trip. He was one of a family of eight brothers, who had been brought up in their younger days around the docks at Sing Sing, now called Ossining. My father was the oldest, and his brothers were, William, Stephen, Ferris, Thomas, George, Samuel, and Charles S., all of whom, at this time, were connected with the building and running of Hudson River sloops and steamboats.

Thomas Collyer was the leading member of this family as a shipbuilder. He went to work as an apprentice to Captain Moses Stanton and worked in his shipyard four years. He then went to work for a Mr. Bergh, the father of Henry Bergh of New York City, who was a shipbuilder. The first sloop that he built was the *First Effort*[1] at Sing Sing; then the *Katrina Van Tassell*, launched in 1838, and which sailed the river until 1883, when she was laid on the beach under the Palisades to die. The first steamboat he built was the *Trojan* at West Troy, and from there he went up to Lake Champlain and built steamers. This was in 1844. Then he went to New York and opened a yard with his brother William, at the foot of 12th Street, East River, New York City. There he built the steamers *Santa Claus*, *Kingston*, and *Niagara*. This partnership was dissolved in 1847, and Thomas Collyer started a yard of his own at the foot of 21st Street, East River, New York City. Here he built the steamers *Armenia*, *George Law*, and *Reindeer* to run

[1] With the aid of his brother William then 14 years old.

Sail vs. Steam

between New York and Albany. He also built the *Daniel Drew* and the steamer *Henry Clay* which was built in 1850, and was burned at Riverdale on July 28, 1852, in which seventy passengers perished. He also built the steamer *Thomas Collyer*, which was the last boat he built before his death. This steamer was later furbished up and sold to John H. Starin, and is now called the *Sam Sloan*, running in the harbor of New York. His records show that he built three sloops, twenty-six barges, four propellers, twelve schooners, three barques, two sailing ships, five steamships, thirty-seven steamboats, and two yachts.

These North River sloops were a great industry on the Hudson River in those days, there being hundreds of them running from the different towns to New York, and from Albany to eastern ports. From Red Hook landing, my father ran the sloops *First Effort* and *Perseverance* as packet sloops, also the sloop *Belle*, built by William Collyer at Green Point for this trade.

The regular sailing time of these sloops was a trip every two weeks from Red Hook to New York and return. These North River sloop boatmen, as they were called in those days, were prominent men, and were the business men of the Hudson valley. They not only had to know how to sail and manage their sloops in all kinds of weather, but also to know the depth of water all along the Hudson, as in those days most of these sloops were keel boats and drew from ten to twelve feet of water.[1] Their captains also had to know good harbors and anchorages, and where the wind from different quarters would be dangerous to navigation of these small vessels. And I might here say, a North River sloop would only carry from fifty to two hundred tons. Their captains, also, had to be good business men, for the captain of a packet sloop took charge of all the farmers' produce, sold the cargo, collected the money, and made the

---

[1] The lights and buoys now numerous, were formerly few and far between.—W. E. V.

Sail vs. Steam

cash return to the farmer when he got home each trip. This was the business of a North River sloop captain, where to-day there is not one to be found on the Hudson in this trade. The principal traffic of the Hudson valley is now being done by steamers towing large scows, barges, and carrying from four hundred to one thousand tons, and by steamboats and railroads carrying the passengers, produce, and general merchandise of the Hudson River towns.

After the Hudson River railroad came through Red Hook, and about 1850 my father sold his storehouse and landing to that company, as the line went directly through his property and took away the dock facilities for the freighting business. Then he engaged in running a small market sloop named the *Rival*, going to Albany and buying his cargo of flour, feed, grain, and different things that would sell in their season to the brickyards and merchants along the Hudson. This was carried on for a number of years with the little sloop

Rival that could carry but fifty tons, but at this time it was a good business.

As the different lines of steamers progressed on the Hudson, and the market for grain got farther west, this business gave out for sloops and schooners, and the *Rival* was sold in 1861 at the beginning of the Civil War.

In the spring of 1865 he again started the sloop business by going to Poughkeepsie and buying the old sloop *Benjamin Franklin*, which was built at Huntington, L. I., in the year 1836. She was owned in Poughkeepsie by a Captain John Van Keuren, and ran from Poughkeepsie to Rondout, carrying coal from Rondout. This sloop could carry eighty-five tons, so you see what a sloop of that size could do to-day in supplying the city of Poughkeepsie with coal. This was my first experience in joining a North River sloop. I went to Poughkeepsie on board the sloop *Benjamin Franklin* as a cabin boy in the spring of 1865. Our first job that went with this sloop was to

SLOOP "BENJAMIN FRANKLIN," WITH CAPTAIN JOHN L. COLLYER ON THE DECK
From a photograph taken at Seabring's dock, Low Point, 1881

carry crockery and earthenware goods from Foster's dock at Poughkeepsie for the firm of Reidinger & Caire, who manufactured these goods at this time at 146 Main Street, Poughkeepsie, from what was called potters' clay. I might here say that this clay was all freighted by sloops from Woodbridge and Cheese Creek, New Jersey, to Poughkeepsie, and then made into this kind of ware, which was distributed along the Hudson. For many years we made these trips both spring and fall, and between these times we ran principally to Albany and river and Sound ports in the lumber trade.

In those days it was not the custom to have your cargo engaged before going to Albany, but to go up with your sloop and have the lumber merchant come and look you up to take a load of lumber for him. I have seen these small vessels lay three and four abreast at the docks in the lumber district at Albany waiting their turn to get to the dock so as to be able to load, and the rate of freight was from $2.00 to $3.50

per thousand, to different Sound ports, where now there is no trade of this kind for any vessel. Another industry for our sloop was to carry coal from Rondout to the different residences located along the Hudson, such as the Livingstons, DePeysters, and Clarksons who lived above Tivoli. They always got their coal in by the cargo for themselves and their help whom they employed. This kept us busy for several months each summer. Another industry for the North River sloop was to carry wood to the brickyards. And brick, flagstone, lime, cement, and pig-iron were the principal cargoes coming down the Hudson to keep these vessels employed. Gathering ice is also a great industry of the Hudson but it has always been carried in barges.

Thus with my brothers, Frank and Robert, we sailed the sloop *Ben Franklin* until 1877, when I left her to join the schooner *Iron Age* and later to be captain of the schooner *Henry B. Fidderman* in the spring of 1878. My

Sail vs. Steam

father sailed the sloop *Ben Franklin* until the time of his death in 1889, when the sloop was sold to do service as a lighter in New York Harbor.

My father's old sloop the *First Effort* already mentioned, met with a singular disaster after he parted with her. While lying at anchor on a dark night near Marlborough, the big steamboat *James W. Baldwin*, mistaking the sloop's lights for those on the wharf where the steamer was to land, came alongside and struck the sloop with such a violent impact that she sank in fifty feet of water. All on board were saved, but the sloop was never raised. The *Baldwin* bore a bad reputation for collisions with sailing craft. She is still on the river but under another name.

I found this statement and account of the first steamboat on the Hudson River among the manuscript papers of Colonel Nathan Beckwith of Red Hook in Dutchess County. He died on the 4th of March, 1865, in the eighty-seventh year of his age.

The first trip of the steamer *Clermont* started from the East River and went to Jersey City. She was constructed under the personal supervision of Robert Fulton in 1807. She was one hundred feet long, twelve feet wide, and seven feet deep. This steamboat made two or three trips to Albany, and was hauled out at Red Hook, near where Herman Hoffman's store stood, which was destroyed by the British in the Revolutionary War. The property is now owned by Mr. DeKoven. In the winter of 1807 said boat was lengthened to one hundred and fifty feet and widened to eighteen feet, the name was changed to *North River*. The hull was built by David Brown of New York, and the engine by Watt and Bolton of England. The following advertisement appeared in the Albany *Gazette*, September 1, 1807: "The steamboat *North River* will leave Paulus Hook, Jersey City, on Friday, September 4th, at nine o'clock A.M. and arrive at Albany on Saturday at nine o'clock P.M. Good berths and accommodations are provided. The charge to each passenger is as follows:—To Newburgh, $3.00, time fourteen hours; to Poughkeepsie, $4.00, time seventeen hours; to Esopus $5.00, time twenty

Sail vs. Steam

hours; to Hudson $5.50, time thirty hours; to Albany $7.00, time, thirty-six hours." A notice in the same paper of October 5, 1807 announces that Mr. Fulton's new steamboat left New York at ten o'clock A.M., against a strong tide and very high water, also a violent gale from the north; it made headway beyond the most sanguine expectations and without being wrecked by the water, heavy sea and gale."

REMINISCENCES OF ACCIDENTS TO SLOOPS

On June 12, 1869, the schooner *Orbit* coming down the river with the wind northwest, loaded with brick, when off Little Stony Point,[1] was struck by a heavy flaw, and before she could come out of it and shake, she ran under, filled and sank. She belonged to Captain Lewis Sheldon and brother, of Fort Montgomery. No one was lost.

On November 20, 1869, there was a terrific gale, east and southeast. Five or six vessels sank at the wharves at Newburgh.

[1] In the Highlands, near Coldspring.—W. E. V.

88 Sloops of the Hudson

The sloop *Quackenbush*, belonging to Capt. E. Kearney of Ulster County, was sunk. She lay at Bigelow's dock, loaded with flagstones. The tug *John Fuller* pumped her out, and she was raised.

On March 26th and 27th, 1870, there was a severe east northeast gale. In Haverstraw bay the effect of the storm was very destructive. Brickyard docks and vessels suffered, there being such a high tide. Ten sloops and schooners were sunk between Haverstraw and Grassy Point. The schooner *Brook*, Captain George Hawkins, loaded with lumber from Newburgh, went ashore above Grassy Point and sank in the same storm.

April 25, 1870, the schooner *Cabinet* of Newport, having loaded coal at Newburgh, while on her way down the river ran on the flats just below Constitution Island. The captain started to run an anchor, not considering the extreme depth

Sail vs. Steam

of the water in the channel, it being from one hundred to one hundred and fifty feet deep. They took their large anchor and chain in the small boat, and the anchor, chain, boat and men all went to the bottom.

In the year 1877, the new terminal of the Newburgh and Fishkill ferry to the N. Y. Central Depot was completed, and in October the ferry commenced to run at this landing.

On June 8, 1878, the sloop *Milan* of Rondout, was beating down, loaded with flagging-stones. The wind was blowing heavily from the south and east, and when off Pollipel's Island, in Newburgh bay, the captain had gone about on the west shore and was standing to the eastward, when there came a heavy puff down from the mountains, striking her dead full, and following the vessel around; the cargo shifted and the vessel filled and sank. She was afterwards raised and rigged into a schooner and called the *George Hurst*.

Sloops of the Hudson

On July 2, 1878, the sloop *Illinois*, then having been altered into a schooner for two years, owned and commanded by Captain James Wilson of Newburgh, while lying at anchor in Long Island Sound in a fog off Captain's Island, was run into by the Stonington Line steamer *Massachusetts*, and sunk. The *Illinois* had left Saybrook the day before the accident, and by the morning of the second, before daylight, got up as far as Captain's Island, wind all died out, ebb-tide made, so they anchored. At three or four o'clock in the morning it set in foggy. At a little after four o'clock, the steamer *Massachusetts* came along and struck the schooner on the starboard quarter a glancing blow, taking the whole side of the vessel out, and she sank. The wreckers went to work and in about thirty hours the vessel was on the ways at City Island. The *Illinois* was originally a packet sloop, running from Newburgh, and was built there at the foot of South Street in 1818. She could carry about one hundred and fifty tons.

Sail vs. Steam

On July 8, 1879, the schooner *Isaac Sherwood*, then belonging to Captain William Bacon of Haverstraw, loaded with brick, had just come off the flats with a nice breeze from the north, and when a little below Grassy Point, met the propeller *John L. Hasbrouck*, of the Poughkeepsie Transportation Company with the Newburgh barge *Charles Spear* alongside in tow. The night was not dark, and the moon was shining. They took a course for each other, the steamer not sheering, nor did the schooner alter her course. The steamer stopped and backed, but too late, for as soon as she commenced to back she struck the schooner just forward of the fore-rigging, cutting in for four feet. The schooner filled immediately and went down in about thirty feet of water. The crew of five men just had time to get into the yawl. The mast and rigging, as she heeled over when she went down, did considerable damage to the propeller's rail.

On August 22, 1879, the sloop *Mary Warner*, belonging to Captain Hiram Meeks, of Fort Montgomery, and carrying brick from Benjamin Walsh's yard at New Windsor, was beating down with a nice breeze and standing to the eastward, when the steam yacht *Nooya*, bound up under a full head of steam, ran into the sloop, striking her on the starboard side, forward of the mast. The yacht being sharp and built of steel, cut half way through the sloop, and she sank immediately. The crew were saved by their yawl. The yacht was very badly damaged and had just time to run ashore at Verplanck's Point, where she filled and settled to the bottom.

From Captain John Pinckney of Low Point, now Chelsea, formerly captain of the schooner *Iron Age*, running from the Manhattan Iron Works at New York for a number of years, I get the following information:

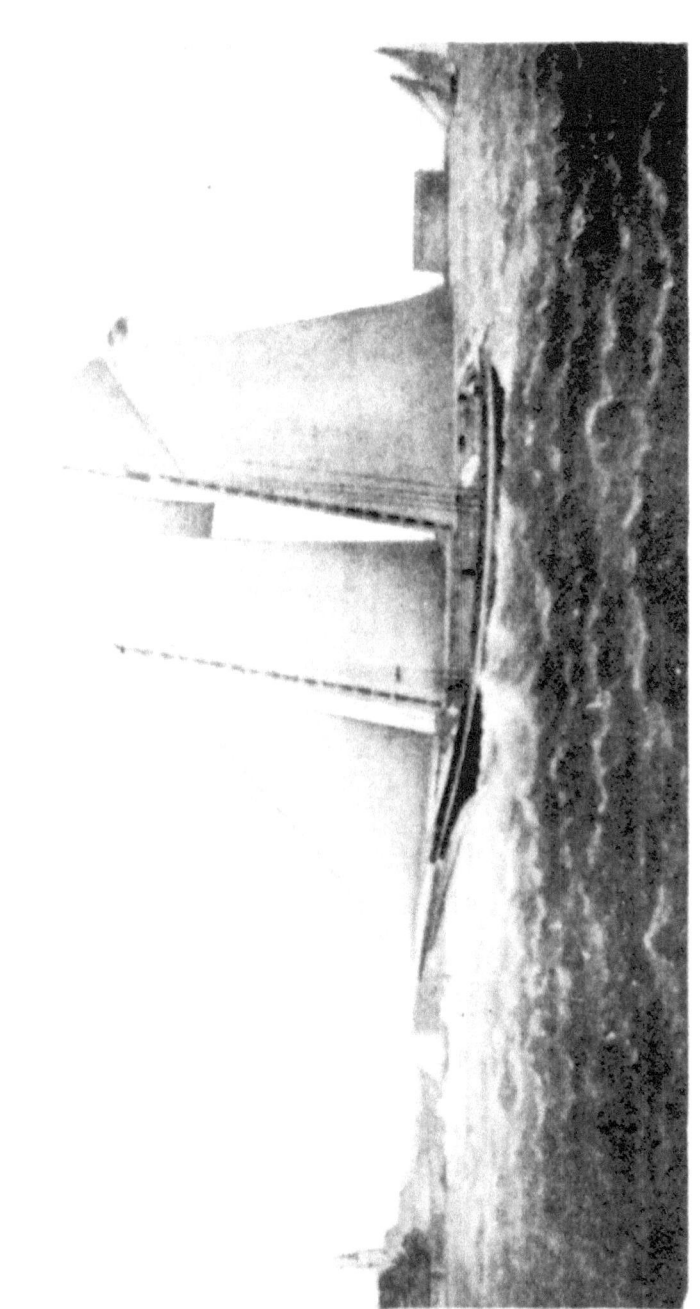

THE SCHOONER "IRON AGE," CAPTAIN JOHN PINCKNEY OF LOW POINT, NOW CHELSEA

From an oil painting

Sail vs. Steam

The first centreboard used on the Hudson River was introduced by Cornelius Carman, who was a builder of sail and steam vessels at Low Point, and was put by him in the sloop *Freedom*.

The first jib-traveller for sloops was invented by David Hunt of Low Point, who was a sloop-boatman from that place and at one time sailed on the packet sloop *Matteawan*, running from there.

The red and green side-lights for sail and steam vessels were first used on the river in 1862, and were introduced by General Benjamin Butler who was interested in a factory that made these lights. They were sold for $25.00 a set.

The first railway for hauling out sloops on the Hudson was put down at Nyack in 1845. Before that time, vessels would go to Cow Bay, Long Island, and other beaches to caulk and paint their bottoms, at the end of the season.

Sloops of the Hudson

A LIST OF SOME OF THE OLD SLOOPS OF THE HUDSON RIVER COMPILED BY CAPT. M. W. COLLYER[1]

Ambassador, of Rondout
Albert Lewis, built in 1861 at Nyack
Asa Bigelow, of Malden
Abraham Cosgrove, of Croton
Anna Van Cortlandt, of Croton
Anna Maria, of Newburgh
Anna V. Willis, of Nyack
Andes
Annie M. Tower, built in 1871 at Poughkeepsie
Adaline Townsend, built in 1854 at Poughkeepsie
Ann Amelia, built in 1827 at Southold, N. J.
Anna Maria, built at Greenport
American System
Anaconda
Addison, built in 1819 at Coxsackie
Abram Jones
Argus
American Eagle,[2] of Haverstraw
Anna Maria No. 2.

[1] The style of the names shows a progression through the sentimental, the patriotic and the political, then to the prosaic, and finally, in the successors to the sloops and schooners, we reach the mere numerical in the big scow-barges which now carry upwards of five hundred tons of brick or crushed stone.—W. E. V.

[2] Built by John I. Woolsey, and was the fastest sloop sailed in Haverstraw Bay.—M. W. C.

Sail vs. Steam

Ariel
Advocate
Abraham Lincoln, built in 1861 at Haverstraw
American Star, built in 1853 at Nyack
Annie E. Leet, built at Greenport, L. I.

Belle, built by Wm. Collyer at Sing Sing, N. Y.
Bucktail[1]
Billow
Benj. Stagg, built in 1839 at Newburgh
Bridgeport, of Poughkeepsie
Benj. Aiken, built in 1836 at Greenbush, N. Y.
Benj. Franklin[2] *No. 2*, built in 1831 at Yonkers
Bolivar, of New Baltimore, N. Y.
Betsey & Ann
Benj. Franklin, built in 1836 at Huntington
Bride, of Cornwall on Hudson
Banner, built in 1859 at Staten Island
Benj. Brandeth, built in 1839 at Sing Sing, by Sniffin
Bronk, built in 1832

---

[1] This was the name applied to the Tammany wing of the Democratic party. The faction was opposed to DeWitt Clinton. A satirical poem called *Bucktail Bards*, aimed at Clinton, was written and published by the late Gulian C. Verplanck in 1819.—W. E. V.

[2] Benjamin Franklin Transportation Co. of Yonkers takes its name from this sloop; she was a packet from Yonkers in 1839. Captain Joseph Peene, her master, was the father of the Peene brothers now operating this line from Yonkers.—M. W. C.

Charles Lynch, of Rondout
Canal, of Rondout
Charles Hadden, built in 1853 at Coxsackie
Carrie Gurnee, formerly *First Effort*, built in 1869 at Rondout, N. Y.
Controller
Contrivance[1] (scow), built in 1818 at Jersey City
Congress, of Rondout
Comet, of Spuyten Duyvil
Cadet (periauger rig[2]), of West Point
Centurion, of Hastings
Capitol, of Malden
Clermont, of Saugerties
Commodore Jones, of Fishkill
Clarissa Ann, of Rondout
Ceres, of Hudson
Comanche
Carver, of Rondout

[1] She was owned by Daniel Tompkins who brought her from Newark, N. J., to Stony Point on Hudson, and used by him in the brick trade, which he established in the neighborhood. The *Contrivance*, though a flat-bottom and scow-model sloop, was a fast sailer. She held the river until 1904, when she was sunk in collision with steamer *James W. Baldwin*, and her captain, Calvin Delanoy, of Glasco, was drowned.—M. W. C.

[2] A term applied on the North River, and perhaps elsewhere, to vessels with two masts, but without bowsprit or headsail. They were generally small. The *Cadet* plied between Newburgh and West Point carrying supplies for the Post. Her master was Capt. Cronk.—W. E. V.

Sail vs. Steam

Charles D. Belding, of Rondout
Celerity, built in 1836 at Nyack
Councillor
Chatham
Convoy, of Nyack
Caroline, of Fishkill owned by J. P. De Wint.
China
Canaan
Congress, built in 1826 at Coxsackie
Clinton, of Glasco
Catskill, of Catskill
Climax

David Belknap, of Newburgh
David Sands,[1] of Newburgh
Diamond State, of Poughkeepsie
Delaware, of Fishkill
David Munn, of Haverstraw
Dart,[2] built at Nyack
Daring, built in 1862 at Poughkeepsie

Exchange,[3] of Newburgh
Eliza Ann
Esmeralda, of Croton

[1] While anchored in New York harbor was run into and sunk by a steamship at night. No one saved but her captain, William Coleman.—M. W. C.

[2] A very smart sloop, owned by Captain Vergil Coleman of Fishkill.—M. W. C.

[3] Owned by Isaac Quick; lost by George Miller at Manhattanville, N. Y.—M. W. C.

Edward Bigelow, of Malden
Eclipse
Exertion, of Haverstraw
Ellen Eliza, of Haverstraw
Emeline [1]
Emma
Ella Jane, of Harlem
Entice

First Effort, built at Sing Sing
Frances Ann
Flash (periauger rig)
Franklin, of Poughkeepsie
Florence
Favorite
Frances Jane
Fame

General Putnam
General Ward, of New Hamburgh
Globe
Grand Council
Green County Tanner, of Catskill
George Law,[2] of Cornwall
General Van Cortlandt, of Croton
Garrett I. Demarest, of Nyack
George M. Dallas, built at Peekskill

[1] *Emeline*, a packet from Yonkers in 1825—Captain Isaac Ruton.—M. W. C.
[2] Carried the stone for High Bridge Aqueduct, New York.—M. W. C.

Sail vs. Steam

General Livingston
General Scott, of Cold Spring
General Green
Glide, of Nyack
Gideon Lee, of Malden
General Montgomery
Gloucester

Henry Edwards, of Newburgh
Hendrickson, of Tarrytown
Hunter (scow-sloop), of Athens
Henry Soudder
Huntress
Henry Barclay, of Poughkeepsie
Hannah Ann, of Glasco
Harriet P. Ogden, of Hudson
Henry Gage

Intrepid, of Highland Falls
Illinois, of Newburgh
Iowa, of Rondout
Independence[1]
Intelligence
Index
Isabella

James Coates, of New Hamburgh
Joseph Hammond, of Cornwall

[1] Captain, John Garrison of Yonkers, who ran her as a packet. Built in 1825.—M. W. C.

John Jay,[1] of Poughkeepsie
James Pollock, of Newburgh
John Marsh, of Wilbur
Jane Grant, of New Hamburgh
Jewel
John Henry
Julia, of Poughkeepsie
John Jones, of Cold Spring
Joseph Moran
John D. Noyells, of Haverstraw
John T. Beveridge, of Newburgh
John L. Richards, of Saugerties
Judge
Jack Downing
James R. Sawyer, of Haverstraw
John I. Woolsey, of Nyack

Kemble, built in 1825 at Poughkeepsie
Kamana
Katrina Van Cortlandt, of Croton
Kentucky
Kinderhook

Little Martha, built in 1867 at New Hamburgh
Lafayette
Luzerne
Lucy Hopkins
Linnet

[1] Later of Newburgh. Captain Isaac Wood was her master.—M. W. C.

Sail vs. Steam

Mohican,[1] built in 1837 at Peekskill
Mary Dallas, of New Hamburgh
Meridian
Michigan
Martin Wynkoop, of Rondout
Mary Warner, of Fort Montgomery
Minnerley, of Rondout
Mary Willis, of Haverstraw
Margaret, built in 1835 at Sing Sing
Mary Kemble
Mad Anthony
Matteawan, of Low Point
Mary Emma (scow), of Cold Spring
Milan, of Rondout
Marshall
Martin Van Buren, of Croton
Mechanic
Martin Hines, of Yonkers
Miracle, of Haverstraw

North America (a scow), of Cornwall
Newburgh, of Newburgh
Nancy
Noah Brown
Ney
Nassau, of Saugerties
New Jersey, of Fishkill

---

[1] Her "bones" lie off my residence at Chelsea and serve as a breakwater.—M. W. C.

102   Sloops of the Hudson

Napoleon
Neptune, of Newburgh

Oregon, of New Windsor
Orbit
Orange Packet, of Newburgh
Oregon No. 3, of Malden
Othello
Ophelia, of Cornwall
Oregon No. 2

Peter R. Valleau, of Poughkeepsie, built in 1829 at Nyack
Progress
Perry Van Cortlandt, of Croton
Pell C. Vought
Pearl
Pilot
Pennsylvania, of Malden
Pelie
Perseverance, of Red Hook
Phœbe Jane Minnerley, of Rondout

Quackenbush

Revenge
Rebecca Ford
Reindeer, of Athens
Ralph Van Houghton
Rising Sun

CAPTAIN JOHN LYON COLLYER LATE OF LOW POINT
From a photograph by F. E. Walker, Fishkill-on-Hudson

Sail vs. Steam

Revenue, of Athens
Rival, of Tivoli
Richard Davis, of Poughkeepsie
Ransom, of Rondout
Robert North

Superior
Star
Samuel A. Cunningham
Samsondale,[1] of Newburgh
Sophia Ann
Swift
Sarah Frances
Samuel Marsh (scow-sloop)
Stephen G. Beekman, built at Nyack
Surprise, of Poughkeepsie
Specia
Spy
Sarah Elizabeth
Speaker
Stamford
Saginaw
Superb

Thomas S. Marvel, of Newburgh
Thomas Webb, of Cold Spring
Temperance
Tremper

[1] Captain George Davis Woolsey, of Newburgh, was master of this sloop.—W. E. V.

Troubler,[1] of Haverstraw
Telegraph
Thomas Adams, of Rondout
Tautemio, of New Hamburgh
Twilight

Utica, of Athens
Unity

Vought
Victorine, of Cold Spring
Victory, of Athens
Victoria

William W. Reynolds, of Poughkeepsie
William Johnston
Wonder
William Robbins
Walter F. Brewster,[2] of Newburgh
William Bridger, of Rondout
William Nelson, of Croton
Westchester
William H. Hawkins, of Newburgh
Warren
Walter Klotts,[3] of Rondout

[1] She turned out to be slow and was often in collision. —W. E. V.

[2] She ran into the Nyack ferry losing her mast and sail which fell over the walking beam. Capt. Geo. D. Woolsey was her master.—M. W. C.

[2] Was burned at Merchants' Stores, Brooklyn, in 1900.—M. W. C.

Sail vs. Steam

Westerlo, of Rondout

Young America

Zenobia

SCHOONERS[1] OF THE HUDSON OF 1865 AND LATER AS RECALLED BY CAPT. M. W. COLLYER

A. J. Williams, 1868, Staten Island
A. O. Zabriskie, 1840, Piermont
Adelaide, Cornwall
Albert G. Lawson, 1868, Newburgh
Allen Gurnee, Rondout
Amos Briggs, 1868, Cornwall
Amos T. Allison, 1853, Nyack
Ann M., Verplanck's Point
Annie, 1864, Glenwood
Annie E. Webb
Armada, Hudson
Athalia, 1884, Newark

Beniah Watson, Cornwall
Buckeye, 1864, Poughkeepsie

C. D. Empson
C. P. Schultze, 1863, Poughkeepsie
Capitol, Malden
Carrie McLane, Fishkill
Catharine Du Bois, Hyler's Landing, 1851
Charles Atkinson, 1862, Haverstraw

[1] Some of these were converted from sloops—M. W. C.

106   Sloops of the Hudson

Charles Kruder, 1873, Haverstraw
Clara Post, Rondout
Clayton
Columbia, Rondout

Daniel Tompkins, Stony Point
Dutchess, Athens

Edward Ivans, Fishkill
Elizabeth Washburn, Haverstraw
Elm City,[1] Newburgh
Emma, Cornwall
Emma I. Southard, Croton
Evelina Ross

Fancy, Low Point
Flying Cloud, Lewisburgh
Francis Corwin, Cornwall
Fred Snow,[2] Piermont

General Torbett, Croton
George A. Brandreth, 1847, Sing Sing
George Hurst, Rondout
George Knapp, Haverstraw
George S. Allison, Stony Point
George S. Wood, Haverstraw
Glide, 1838, Nyack
Green County Tanner,[3] 1832, Catskill

[1] Owned at one time by Homer Ramsdell of Newburgh.—M. W. C.
[2] Joseph Tate, captain.—M. W. C.
[3] She was originally a sloop.—M. W. C.

Sail vs. Steam

Hannah E. Brown [1]
Henrietta Collyer, Low Point
Henry B. Fidderman [2]
Henry Clay, 1838
Henry Remsen, 1851, Red Bank
Henry Wardell, 1862, Haverstraw
Hester, Poughkeepsie
Honora Butler, Haverstraw

Iris, New Hamburgh
Iron Age, Low Point
Isaac W. Sherwood, Haverstraw
Isles of Pine, Rondout

James Bolton
Jane N. Ayers, Fishkill
Jane Grant, Rondout
John Brill, Fishkill
John Forsythe, Rondout
John Gould, West Camp
John Jay
John Jones, Cold Spring
John R. Britt, Newburgh
Joseph Hammond, Cornwall
Josie Crowley
Juliette Terry, Kingston
Justus C. Earl, Rondout

[1] Built in 1871 at Newburgh; still running on the river.—M. W. C.

[2] The first vessel of which Moses W. Collyer became master. She was about 90 tons' capacity.—W. E. V.

Sloops of the Hudson

Kate & Mary, Rondout

Lewis R. Mackey [1]
Libbie Worthley, Low Point
Lizzie A. Tolles
Lottie & Annie, Haverstraw
Lucien, Newburgh
Lucy Gurnee, Rondout
Lydia White, Low Point

Mad Anthony, Haverstraw, built 1816
Manchester & Hudson, Rondout
Marcus L. Ward
Maria, Haverstraw
Maria Hearn, Fishkill (see footnote 2, page 110)
Marion (scow-schooner), Cold Spring
Matthew B. Vassar, Poughkeepsie, built 1855
Minerva, Hudson
Minnie C. Post, Rondout
Missouri, Cold Spring

Nellie Bloomfield, Newburgh
Nicholas Meyerhoff, Croton
Noah Brown
Norma, Cold Spring

Oliver H. Booth, 1856, Poughkeepsie
Oregon No. 2

Potter & Hooper, Haverstraw

[1] Was a very fast sailer—M. W. C.

Sail vs. Steam

Rebecca & Eliza, Newburgh
Richard Washburn, Haverstraw
Richmond, of Poughkeepsie
Robert A. Forsythe,[1] Newburgh
Robert Blair, Haverstraw
Robert Knapp, Haverstraw

Sally M. Adkins
Sarah Jane Gurnee, Rondout
Sarah Quinn
Seabird, Sing Sing
Shamrock, Haverstraw
Sharpshooter

T. W. Spencer, Cornwall
The Florence, Haverstraw
Thomas I. Southard
Thomas J. Owen, Verplanck's Point
Thomas Jefferson, Fishkill
Timothy Wood, Rondout
Trimmer, Malden

Uriah F. Washburn,[2] Haverstraw

[1] Built in 1866 at Newburgh, and ran from there to Albany, carrying lumber and merchandise. Her captain and owner was Ambrose Bradley. who had the record of owning a greater variety of vessels than any other man on the river. His brother was John Bradley of Low Point.—M. W. C.

[2] Built in 1866 at Tompkins Cove by Jake Woolsey. —M. W. C.

Warren, Verplanck's Point
William A. Ripley, Low Point
William E. Peck, Haverstraw
William H. Barnes, Haverstraw
William H. Camp,[1] Newburgh
William H. Harrison
William M. Evarts, West Camp
William Mayo, Mayo
Wm. Voorhis

The Hudson river builders of some of these sloops and schooners were:

Timothy Wood, Milton
John I. Woolsey,[3] Haverstraw
Jacob Woolsey, Tompkins Cove
Thomas S. Marvel, Newburgh and Cornwall
George Polk, Poughkeepsie
Henry Rodiman, Cornwall
James P. Voorhis, Nyack
Thomas Collyer, Sing Sing
William Collyer, Sing Sing
John Felter, Nyack
John G. Perry, Nyack

[1] Captain Hank Wilson.—M. W. C.
[2] Was sunk at West Point by steamer *Alicia Washburn*, in the deepest water of the Hudson, which is 225 ft. Her captain was John Paye of Fishkill.—M. W. C.
[3] Built also the *Victorine*, *Wanderer*, *American Eagle*, all very fast sloops.—M. W. C.

Bulman & Brown, Newburgh
David Sands, Milton
Cornelius Carman,[1] Low Point
William Dickey, Nyack
Jefferson McCausland, Rondout
Morgan Everson, Rondout
Nicholas Clair, Malden
Deacon Dorwin, New Windsor

[1] Inventor of the centreboard.

PART III

PERSONAL REMINISCENCES OF CAPTAIN GEORGE D. WOOLSEY [1]

I BECAME quite familiar with the names of the packet sloops sailing from Newburgh, for at this time, 1825, my father was captain of the packet sloop *Illinois* running from Newburgh to New York, carrying passengers and produce from the farms and sailing from David Crawford's wharf at Newburgh.

[1] George Davis Woolsey was born at Poughkeepsie on the 12th day of October, 1829, and died at Newburgh on the 23d day of March, 1900. He married Timna Quick of Milton-on-Hudson. They had four children: Charles D., who died in infancy; Charles C., Anna H., now Mrs. Cosman, and Harriet, now Mrs. Garner. Mrs. Woolsey, the widow, is now living on Grand Street, Newburgh.

The manuscript from which these reminiscences were taken was in a fragmentary condition when Mrs. Woolsey gave it to Capt. M. W. Collyer for publication. So much as appears here is all that was available or deemed germane to the subject of this book.—W. E. V.

CAPTAIN GEORGE DAVIS WOOLSEY LATE OF NEWBURGH
Reproduced from an old print

There were also the sloops *Favorite*, 1825, *Orange Packet*, 1825, *Eclipse*, 1825, *James Monroe*, 1830, *Meridian*, 1835, *David Belknap*, 1838, *Benjamin Stagg*, 1838, and the *John Beveridge*,[1] 1838. The greater number of these vessels, with many others were built here at the village of Newburgh, and at Sand's dock, Milton, before my recollection. However, they were in use, and employed in the freight and passenger business from Newburgh, some of them before, and some after my coming on the scene of action. Mr. Samuel Wood, a man who belonged to a family of shipbuilders, conducted the business at or near the foot of South Street, then called Academy Hill. He being an uncle of my father, by marrying Grandfather Woolsey's sister, has given me this information. Also, I have known his only son, who was quite a prominent and successful business man in New York City until his death in the fifties.

[1] Named from a brewer of Newburgh, whose ale was known throughout the State.—W. E. V.

There was a brother also, named Timothy Wood, conducting the ship-building, either at Athens or Coxsackie. I remember of one of the up-river packets being named *Timothy Wood* in his honor.

All of the vessels built in those early days were very sharp, much dead rise, deep keel, with great draught of water. For vessels of their carrying capacity, the *Illinois* with a capacity of about 135 or 140 tons, when loaded, had a draught of about twelve feet. Having a deep keel running the whole length of the vessel, and of much greater depth aft than forward, the man who was in command, or sailing master of these packets must necessarily be well acquainted with navigation on the river, conversant with all the shoals, sand-bars, rocks, and obstructions, so as to keep them from grounding and make their trips regularly, for they were advertised to sail on certain days from Newburgh, and also from New York.

The old packet *Illinois*, as we first remember her construction, had a cabin about half the length of the vessel for the accommodation of passengers, two after-cabins or state-rooms, altogether in both cabins some twenty-six or twenty-eight berths. The cabin was built of hard wood, much of it mahogany, with a very large oval mirror across the bulkhead, separating the main cabin from the state-rooms aft. Panels composed of mahogany, mirrors in panels at head of berths, with goldbead around. She had a very long companion-way, with large brass signal lamp hanging in the centre for light at night, and a floor of hard wood, kept very white and clean. Everything then known for the comfort of the passengers was done that could be done. There was nearly as much preparation to go to New York then on a packet, as people make now to go to Europe. The women brought their sewing to fill up their time industriously, for at times in very dull weather, the packets would be some two days on the passage. The hold of the packets was always divided by separate bins for the different kinds of grain and produce brought by the farmers. What was termed the forecastle, the place set apart for culinary purposes, was arranged much after the manner of the houses of that day, having a chimney and fireplace of brick, also a mantel over the fireplace, and a brick hearth in order to keep the vessel from fire. There were four berths also in the forecastle for the accommodation of the men on the vessel. Frequently we would have the *Illinois* loaded decks to the water, especially in the fall; hold full of all kinds of grain; the long quarter-deck filled with butter, dead hogs, and often I have seen a sheep-pen around where we used to steer, full of sheep, which made it nice and warm for the man at the helm in cold weather. Frequently we would have live-stock on the main deck, lashed to a pole running fore and aft from mast to quarter-deck. In fact the business, if my memory serves rightly, increased wonderfully, so that I have seen all kinds of produce in wagons, waiting for their turn to be un-

Capt. Woolsey's Reminiscences

loaded, standing from Crawford's dock up into Water Street, for some distance, and when the packets were thus so full and heavily loaded, they were towed to New York, for there were steamboats also, of the first old type, running from Newburgh at that time, which we will mention in their proper place.

The water-front of the village of Newburgh, was very different from the way it is now situated—the docks having all been extended out into the river. Once we had twenty-five to thirty-five feet of water all along the east side of Front Street, having seen the whaling ships laying where the Erie Freight Depot and office now are. The *Highlander*, when she first came, about 1834 or 1835, had her dock at the south side of First Street, where the public sheds now are. B. Carpenter's dock on the same line of Front Street, foot of Carpenter Street. At the foot of First Street was a slip, where John McCormic kept boats to let. Every available space along the docks was used for ranks of wood piled there for the use of the steamboats, as they all used wood for steaming purposes, there then being no anthracite coal.

The *Illinois* used to lay where Cameron's lumber office now is. There was a short pier built out where the Long Dock now is, for the Albany boats to land at. The Newburgh and Fishkill ferry, under its present effective and efficient management, has become the most perfect system of ferriage to accommodate the public, outside of New York City. Our ferry system and its environments have indeed kept pace with the growth and prosperity of the city. Its progress and advance date back in my time, since its purchase by Mr. Thomas Powell, about 1835. Mr. David Crawford also extended a dock out from the foot of Third Street about 1836 or 1837, for the opposition boats running from New York to Albany to land at. The next dock north of and adjoining David Crawford's, was called DeWint's dock, where a packet

Capt. Woolsey's Reminiscences

sailed from. Then came the Oakley and Davis dock, which was the last and the farthest north of the regular packet and steamboat docks in the freighting and forwarding business between the village and New York City.

While I am giving an account of my recollections of the old sloop packets running from the village of Newburgh, probably it will not be out of place here to mention the fact, that a few years before my time a sloop met with a very serious and disastrous accident. It was the sloop *Neptune*. The accident caused such a gloomy and melancholy feeling through the village and county, that it was some time before it was forgotten; in fact, I remember its being often referred to by the men on the vessels and others. If I remember the account correctly, it happened in this manner: About 1824 or 1825, late in the fall, about the time when we often have heavy northwest winds, which make it very dangerous navigating through the Highlands, the sloop left New York with about fifty tons of plaster, some of it on deck, also quantities of goods for stores. There were some fifty or fifty-five passengers, men, women, and children also on the packet. If I rightly heard the account, the captain, whose name was Halstead, remained in New York, as they frequently did, to settle up and collect bills. The man in charge, or sailing-master of the packet was John Decker, whom I well knew, for after the unfortunate accident he never could get any other position as sailing-master on the packets or vessels, and he took up the business of cartman in New York, where I frequently saw him in my time, as he used to cart produce from the *Illinois* and other packets. He was a very tall and powerfully built man, about six feet two or three inches tall, high cheek-bones, very large bones, hands large and drawn somewhat out of shape, eyes small and red, or bloodshot. He was rather a remarkable appearing man, I being young, and knowing of the prevailing talk about

Capt. Woolsey's Reminiscences

him, caused me to notice him particularly, and was so impressed by his peculiar look, I can thus describe him.[1]

The packet came through the lower part of the river all right, although it was blowing very heavy and puffy. Coming around West Point it could be seen from Cold

---

[1] This disaster took place in the most dangerous part of the Worragat or Werrygut, (there is no settled spelling). Perhaps the name is derived from the Dutch word *Weer*, weather, and *Gat*, a hole or gut. This reach extends from Pollipel's Island, off Storm King, southward to Constitution Island, opposite West Point, a distance of about four miles. When the wind is south or north—that is, parallel with the course of the river, no difficulty is experienced by sailing vessels, no matter how fresh it blows. It is the westerly winds, either N.W. or S.W., that cause trouble. For instance, a sloop may be close-hauled passing through Newburgh Bay, beating down against a fresh southwester. Before Cornwall is reached the sheets can be started, and as she passes into the Worragat the wind will be fair, with occasional heavy flaws from the west, and I have even had to jibe back and forth when passing Little Stony Point. The fair wind holds until West Point is reached, then it becomes dead ahead to the north end of the Race. Here the wind is fair again, which will carry the sloop out of the Highlands, past Verplanck's and Stony Points, and into the broad waters of Haverstraw Bay and Tappan Zee where it is plain sailing again.—W. E. V.

Spring up through to Pollipel's Island that the heavy puffs were very dangerous, therefore requiring the utmost skill in navigating and handling the vessel. When off Little Stony Point where, when blowing from the northwest, there is always much heavier gusts of wind than anywhere else in the Highlands, as the wind comes rushing down through the low valley between Storm King and the Crow's Nest on the south (what we then used to call Mother Cronk's Cove) the wind often comes with such force that it picks the water up as it comes, but it always gives warning, for you can see the impression on the water, and hear the roar as it comes. Then the careful navigator, with good judgment, will be prepared to meet it by having good steerage way on his vessel, and getting the head-sail in before it strikes the vessel. It appears by the account, that Decker had the *Neptune* double-reefed at the time, but did not get in the head-sail, therefore when the heavy squall struck the packet she went over and down so low that the plaster shifted, and into the forecastle companionway, which was forward and on the starboard side, the water began to rush and she filled and sunk. Out of the fifty or fifty-five passengers and the crew, I believe there were but sixteen or eighteen saved. I think that the late Levi D. Woolsey was on board and was saved. The late Captain John Polhemus had a brother, Jacob Polhemus, who was employed on the packet, and was drowned in trying to save a lady. I remember that his widow afterwards married a Judge Bates, who resided on Montgomery Street, between Fourth and Fifth streets.

This serious accident was long remembered and talked of in the village. The *Neptune* was raised and sold off to the east end of Long Island, at Sag Harbor, a port where whale ships were owned and fitted out; also, they discharged their oil there instead of going to New York with it. The owners bought the *Neptune*, and she was kept in the business of carrying hogsheads and barrels of oil from Sag Harbor to New York for years afterwards, as I have frequently seen her coming into New York, loaded with oil. I think she was kept carrying oil until the business of bringing oil to Sag Harbor ceased.

Formerly the business of freighting and forwarding on the River and Long Island Sound was done exclusively by sailing vessels or packets, as they were called, before and about the time the first steamboats were built. Steam was destined to make and produce a great change in the affairs and business on both water and land. As steamboats began to be built, multiply, and increase in numbers and efficiency, they were in a few years much improved from those built before my time. I remember most of the first steamboats built for and employed on the River. They were still in active service when I came on the scene of action. Some of those first old steamers were bought and used in conjunction with the packets

Capt. Woolsey's Reminiscences 125

here at Newburgh, in carrying the produce and passengers to New York. Probably twenty-five or twenty-six years had intervened from the first steamboat, the *Clermont*, in 1807 or 1808, up to the standpoint which I take. During the interval there had been quite a number of steamboats built. The *Providence*, one of the first built for use between New York and Providence, was soon superseded, and her place taken by something superior which, if I am rightly informed, was the *Chancellor Livingstone* and the *United States*, and they also, in due time, the same as the *Providence* were transferred to the Hudson River. The steamboat *Providence* in conjunction with the sloops *Favorite* and the *James Monroe* made their regular trips from Oakley and Davis's dock, for it must be remembered that the business at that time was done from Newburgh, controlling a vast extent of territory, Orange County, the lower part of Ulster, Sullivan, and Delaware counties.

Captain Levi D. Woolsey was captain of

the *Providence*. Having been personally acquainted with Captain Woolsey, and often conversed with him in regard to his early days and life, I remember him as a man of firm decision of character, strictly on the line of justice and equity, careful, also watchful in his business relationship. His branch of the Woolsey family, like all of that name in this country, came from one original stock, who came to this country in 1623 and settled at Flushing, Long Island, where they owned a plantation and were established. From this head or stock came the numerous branches of the Woolsey family. The branch to which Captain Levi D. Woolsey and Captain Elijah L. Woolsey belonged, settled in Ulster County, from whence have come numerous descendants. Captain Woolsey lived to an advanced age, residing at Newburgh with his children until he died in the year 1888, having been born in 1800.

From David Crawford's dock sailed the *Illinois*, of which Captain John Polhemus

Capt. Woolsey's Reminiscences 127

was at first master, and in 1835 succeeded by Captain Elijah L. Woolsey, the steamboat *Baltimore*, Captain Robert Wardrop, was in conjunction, making trips regularly Wednesday from Newburgh and Saturday from New York. Often the packet had so much freight, it was necessary to be towed by the steamer. At Benjamin Carpenter's dock, which was the first dock south of the ferry, the steamboat *William Young* made regular trips once a week. The captain of this steamer, I believe, was named Halstead, not the Captain Charles Halstead of later years, but the one who was captain of the sloop *Neptune* at the time of her capsizing some years before off Little Stony Point.

I do not remember any packet in conjunction with the steamer *William Young*. The steamer *James Madison*, Captain Perry, about the year 1836 or 1837 was built to take her place, and the *William Young* was then taken to Low Point and commenced freighting from there, if memory serves rightly, in the place of the sloop packet *Matteawan*. About this time also, I remember there was a change at David Crawford's dock. The steamboat *Washington* had been built to take the place of the steamer *Baltimore*. Captain Charles Johnston was the first captain of the steamer *Washington*. He was the son of the Rev. John Johnston, who was so long pastor of the First Presbyterian Church in the village. Some few years before these new steamers came to Newburgh, a Captain Chase had the sloop *Eclipse*, running regularly to New York from De Wint's dock, just north of D. Crawford's dock, and about the year 1838 or 1839 the sloop *David Belknap* was built to take the place of the sloop *Eclipse*. Captain Simonson was her captain. They also had the steamboat *Norfolk*, Captain Charles Johnston having become associated with Captain Simonson, commanded the steamer *Norfolk*. The sloop *David Belknap* was frequently towed by the *Norfolk*. I remember that the *David Belknap* was a few years after sold

Capt. Woolsey's Reminiscences

to parties in New York and converted into a schooner, she being staunch, well-built, of good shape and dimensions, heavily timbered, thoroughly treenailed and fastened. She was used a number of years as a coasting vessel and regular packet from New York to Charleston and Savannah, as I frequently saw her after, in that business, laying at or near Pier 8 or 10 East River, discharging and receiving freight for Southern coastwise ports.

Before Captain Simonson became associated with Captain Charles Johnston in business at De Wint's dock, about the year 1835 or 1836, he was captain of the sloop *Meridian*, then running from Oakley and Davis's dock. This firm having disposed of the steamboat *Providence*, had the steamer *Superior*, Captain James H. Leeds, running also to New York.

There was a steamboat running from either De Wint's or Oakley and Davis's dock later on, say from 1838 to 1840, by the name of *General Jackson*. I remember her running from Newburgh, but cannot fairly say where from. At the south part of the village, adjoining the Whaling Dock on the north, Thomas Powell & Company had a line for freight and passenger boats to New York, but I do not remember their having any sloop packets. The first steamboat which I call to mind of theirs was the *Highlander*, which was built expressly for this company at Philadelphia about the year 1834 or 1835. She was greatly in advance and superior to all other steamers then built. She had the same old style of square stern which at that time was so much in vogue. In a few years, however, the designers overcame and gave a more symmetrical shape to the stern and after part of the steamers. The steamers of former build were full forward, having much the shape of the sailing vessels, but the *Highlander* was quite different, having a sharp bow, and carrying this sharpness well aft. She also had more shear than they had formerly given to the steamers.

Her engine was more powerful, having a walking-beam, but I cannot say how much stroke, but it was more than usual. She made the passage to New York in better time than the former boats, say some five hours. She had more steam room also, having two boilers, one on each side of the boat. The accommodation for passengers had been greatly increased. On the whole the *Highlander* was much in advance of the former steamers. When she first came to Newburgh the steamers still used wood for steaming purposes, but it was not long after she came that anthracite coal was discovered, and soon brought to market by the Delaware and Hudson Canal Company in large lumps, just as taken from the mines, therefore the people who used it, had to break it up small for use.

Steamers rapidly increased in number both on Long Island Sound and the Hudson River. I will mention others of the old ones, as they were familiar to me, having seen the most of them, and those which I have not seen, I was conversant with by hearing others discuss their merits, good qualities and speed, for it was expected that every new steamer that came out was to be superior to the last, especially in speed. My father, Captain Elijah L. Woolsey, who often told us of his early life, commenced business on the river on the packet sloop *Intelligence*, from New Paltz, now called Highland, some time before I was born, sailing from there some few years. He afterwards engaged with Richard Davis & Sons, who owned what they called the Lower Dock at Poughkeepsie, carrying on the freighting business very extensively. They had one of the largest, and as was conceded at that time and for years after, the fastest vessel afloat. She was named the *Richard Davis*, after the senior owner of the concern. She was a surprise and a wonder to all who went on the water. My father sailed her for some years, and while he was on this packet from Poughkeepsie I first saw the light, and was named for or by, one of the sons, George Davis Woolsey. The Davises were progressive people, and up to the times, and therefore in due time they sold the packet, *Richard Davis*, and bought the steamboat, *Lady Richmond*, on which my father was pilot. I have heard him tell of going down with her in December, probably the last trip for that year, loaded very deep with produce, especially tons of poultry and game. The ice cut the oakum or caulking out of the seams, and it was leaking so badly they had to put her ashore just below Tarrytown, where she filled, and much of her valuable cargo was lost or destroyed. The old packet *Richard Davis* was still in use in my time. I remember her being rebuilt somewhere up the river, and had her name changed to *James Haddon*.

There was a number of steamers built for Long Island Sound, run there a few years, and then transferred to the River. Whether the *Lady Richmond* was one of those, I cannot say, but the *Philadelphia* and *United States* both were, and transferred to the Hudson River and put on the night line between New York and Albany, calling the *Philadelphia* the *New Philadelphia*, landing at Newburgh where the Long Dock is. Old Mr. Casterline was the general agent at Newburgh. Both vessels were afterwards used as towboats, towing from New Brunswick. The *Philadelphia* being in use the longest time. The *United States* was broken up about 1840.

There was an opposition line also landing at Mr. David Crawford's dock, the *Ohio* with two walking-beams, two separate engines, the *Constitution* and *Constellation*. This opposition was a night line also. The day line of steamers from New York to Albany were the *Novelty* and *Champion*, two fast boats for their day. The steamer *Albany* was afterwards on the day line to Albany. She had a beam-engine, with increased speed and power, and was rebuilt in the year 1837 or 1838, with quite a long, low false stern, carrying a yawl-boat turned bottom up on it. The *Champlain* and *Erie* were, as near as I can remember, kept on the day line from New York to Albany until about the year 1842.

I must not omit to notice the Swiftsure Line running from Albany. I remember their boats very clearly, having often seen them—the *Commerce*, the *Swiftsure*, and the *Oliver Ellsworth*. All of them had crosshead engines. They all towed what they called safety-barges, carrying freight and passengers. I think the object of towing the safety-barges was, as they claimed, the greater safety of the property and passengers entrusted to them. They all became towboats on the river. The *Oliver Ellsworth* was cut through in Newburgh bay by the ice, some years ago, and was run ashore and sunk just below the Danskammer. The *Commerce* was rebuilt in the year 1855, name changed to *Ontario*, and used as a tow-boat until late years. The *Swiftsure* was worn out some years before. About this time the steamer *De Witt Clinton* was running on the night line to Albany, but

I do not remember which line she belonged to. However, some time in the forties she was dismantled, her hull used as a barge, her engine, which was a good one, placed in a new hull, and, if I remember rightly, she was then named the *Knickerbocker*.

There were opposition lines of steamers also on Long Island Sound. There had been large sloop and schooner packets running from all of the principal places, like Bridgeport, New Haven, up the Connecticut to Hartford, New London, Providence, and Fall River. I have some of the packets now in mind, and they were staunch and splendid vessels, running to New York. There were regular packets also established, running from Albany to all of the Eastern ports and cities of any size. They always loaded to their fullest capacity with feed, flour, and all kinds of produce. Albany was a lively, teeming city at that time, vessels laying six to eight abreast, especially in the fall months. Plenty of freight, many anxious to get vessels to load for all ports on the

Capt. Woolsey's Reminiscences 137

River or Sound, paying excellent prices. But the change came on Long Island Sound, the same as on the Hudson, by the introduction of steam and steamboats. It came somewhat slower to the East than on the River. The Eastern people were more attached to their vessels. Also, the vessels at that time were considered more safe to carry their goods and produce, as they were thought more seaworthy than the steamers that were then built. It must be remembered that the steamboat of fifty or sixty years ago was a very crude affair, in an unfinished, rough state, to what they became afterwards. The elements were also much greater to contend with on the Sound and down the coast around Point Judith, and also to New Bedford and Boston.

I suppose there are many alive to-day who remember the terrible, unfortunate accident on January 13, 1840, in a blinding, northeast snow-storm, when somewhere between Oldfield Light and Horton's Point the steamboat *Lexington*, with many passengers on, and loaded with store goods and numerous bales of cotton, bound from New York to Providence, caught fire, burned up, and with no help for the unfortunate people on board. But three or four were saved of all the souls on board, and those endured the elements and suffered worse than death, lashed to a bale of cotton, and were for hours adrift and were not rescued, and finally went ashore on the Long Island shore. There was one of the Woolsey family on board and lost, who lived at Norwich, Connecticut, and left a widow and seven children. This accident, I remember, cast a gloom over all, and was much conversed about through this section of the country.

On the opposition line between New York and Providence, was the steamboat *John W. Richmond*, which was built about the year 1838. She was of an improved type, something superior to the *Lexington*, which had been built some years before. The name of this steamer brings to my recol-

Capt. Woolsey's Reminiscences 139

lection a peculiar and singular incident which I will relate. About the year 1800, and some years after, there was living in the city of Providence a very prominent and influential citizen who was a leader in the city's municipal affairs. He also was a popular and successful physician, having acquired a competency; he having stock in the opposition line, this steamer, *John W. Richmond*, was named for him. He had also in his possession much of the State of Rhode Island's Revolutionary Debt, in bonds and stocks. I frequently, when on my trips eastward, bound around Point Judith, would stop at Stonington, a city at the east end of Fisher's Island Sound, near the state line of Rhode Island and Connecticut, it being the terminus of the Stonington line of steamers, connecting by railroad to Providence, Boston, or any points eastward. In thick, foggy weather it was very convenient to stop there; although the harbor is not so large, it is quite safe, having a good breakwater on the west, which has been greatly improved since I have been down that way, the government has extended it much further to the south, out in the Sound, and made it higher. The holding-ground, or anchorage, is very good indeed, so that in ordinary weather it is a good harbor for vessels that are not too large. On one of my many trips eastward about the year 1874, it being very thick weather, I stopped at Stonington, as was my custom, as I had leisure. It also being my custom to see what I could learn, I wandered off in the suburbs of the city, near the State line, I came across an old burial place which had been used by the people of Stonington for many years; in fact, it was selected as the first burial place for the town. A few years before 1874, as the town had grown to a city and the population increased, they bought other grounds situated in a different section, and rural and modern in appearance. In the old grounds I saw but one tall white marble shaft and the only one in the old place, my curiosity led me to go and examine it, and I found this inscription on one of the four sides:

"Henrietta Richmond, wife of John W. Richmond, born November 29th, 1782, died July 17th, 1849." On the opposite side of the shaft was this inscription, "Doctor John W. Richmond, born September 25th, 1775, died March 4th, 1857. When Rhode Island by her legislation from 1844 to 1850 repudiated her Revolutionary Debt, Doctor Richmond removed from that state to this Borough, and selected this as his family burying place, unwilling that the remains of himself and family should be disgraced by being a part of the common earth of a repudiating state."

On the other two sides of the shaft was an inscription of the birth and death of his children, which I did not copy. It appears, as I was informed afterwards, that he had some ten or twelve thousand dollars of the State of Rhode Island's Revolutionary script or certificates, and during these years mentioned, between 1844 and 1850, he had been offered fifty cents on the dollar for them, but refused to take it, and when the State repudiated the whole debt, he of course, lost all, so he would not be disgraced by being buried in the soil of a repudiating State.

My many calls at Stonington for a harbor, caused me to become well acquainted with many of her first and influential citizens. Many old, retired sea-captains and sailors, especially those having been in and on whaling vessels for years had gained a competency and lived there. One sailor in particular, who had spent the most and the younger part of his life on whaling ships fitting out at New London, I became very intimate with indeed, and we were near and familiar associates and friends. His name was Captain George S. Brewster, living in a beautiful mansion that was situated on raised ground, near the water, having a clear view of the harbor, Fisher's Island Sound, Watch Hill, and the Atlantic Ocean east of Montauk Point, in clear weather. A very fitting place for an old sea-captain who had been tossed about by old Neptune, and who had weathered many a rough sea, to spend the few remaining days that he, through the kindness of Providence, had allotted to him, for Captain Brewster was a very old man when I first met him about the year 1870, being not far from seventy-eight years of age. I had learned to love him because he had a firm, peculiar character and will, and this will controlled a deep sense of justice, right doing, and equity, no selfishness or prejudiced ideas, but gentleness, with charity and love for all. Whether others differed with him in opinion, or not, his kindness was always most prominent; he was the type of a true, honest, Christian man.

In order to give to those who peruse these reminiscences of my life, an intelligent idea of the childlike simplicity, the wholehearted Christian love that controlled the old sailor, I will quote the last paragraph, or closing part of the last letter which I received from the old sailor in the year 1878,

January 14th, for he did not live long after this letter was written:

"We will remember you in our prayers, that you may be blessed and kept; never pass us by without calling, if you can possibly do so without neglect of duty. We shall all be so glad to see you, and all send kind Christian salutations. Make my house your home whenever you come this way. Dear wife and Minnie send love and good wishes, with an interest in your prayers. God bless you and yours."

I know that there was no deceit, dissembling, or hypocrisy about this old friend and sailor. As far as my observation goes, this type of true Christian manhood is in the past and obsolete. Before I close the narrative of Captain Brewster, I will relate as briefly as possible the manner of my first acquaintance with him. On one of my trips, bound eastward around Point Judith, it being thick weather the last of the week, I stopped for a harbor at Stonington. I recollect I went ashore on Sunday morning to find a meeting of some kind. In wandering along the Main Street, out towards the Point where the lighthouse stood, I came to a house or little chapel with this inscription on the doors, "Holiness to the Lord," and on the windows was written the time of preaching and the time of their social meetings. As I approached, there was an old man sweeping the dust and dirt from the stoop. He perceiving me to be a stranger, also a man engaged on the water, for they always can detect each other, saluted me in a very pleasant and kindly manner. There was not a very lengthy conversation, before we commenced to understand each other; the result was that I became acquainted with the little society, and often visited them afterwards, always making his home my home when in the harbor, and many pleasant scenes and incidents occurred when there. The little company of, say fifty to sixty-five, had been Baptist, which was the principal denomination in Stonington, the old sailor being one of the elders and leaders of the Church, but somehow or in some way they had been led into the Second Advent doctrine, which is so prominent and forcibly taught in the Scriptures by Christ Himself, and all of the Apostles and Prophets, many of them pointing to the time of His (Christ's) presence, and the work to be accomplished at that time. This little society of believers were honest and devoted people, and I, then, not perceiving and understanding the teaching of Scripture on this doctrine as it has been revealed and shown to me since, can see now very plainly that they did not at that time comprehend or understand the Scriptural teaching of the manner of His (Christ's) coming or presence, nor the object of his coming; for to this world it will be one of the greatest, the grandest events that the world can conceive of, as it will be a complete revolution, a change of government, social, political and religious or ecclesiastical; the government is to be upon His (Christ's) shoulders, old things are to pass away.

"Behold, I will make all things new; Thy kingdom come, Thy will be done on the earth," so there must be a turning around—a revolution in due time, when the transfer is made and completed; and if God's word is true and not false, it is sure to come, and I hope, in the near future. So I see now, what I did not then, that those devoted people were blinded in respect to the manner and object of the coming and presence of the Son of Man.

The old sailor's death, I was informed by old Captain Tribble of New London, was singular and remarkable, and was in this way: he was looked up to as the father of the little society, therefore their councillor and guide; he, on a certain evening, in one of their social meetings was discoursing on the Scriptures and the precious promises therein, in order to strengthen their faith and hopes for the future. While talking he was suddenly overcome with heart-failure, and dropped to the floor unconscious, and in a few seconds was dead;

thus passing away peacefully and as he thought, in the service of the Truth.

Returning again to my recollections of the steamers of the forties, fifty or sixty years ago, my mind refers back to a class of steamers greatly improved, and much in advance of those I have mentioned. A class of steamers brought forward to a higher rate of speed by the wonderful improvement in machinery and boilers, also by knowledge and instruction gained experimentally in the art of shipbuilding; for about this time there was a complete advancement in the shape, length, symmetry and commodious plans of these steamers. A few which now come to my remembrance, I will mention, such as the *Swallow*, *Rochester*, *South America*, *North America*, *Utica*, *Robert L. Stevens*, not leaving out the old *Norwich*, for she is still in existence and in everyday use, having been used as a tow-boat since 1850. Her hull and shape appeared to be well-formed and adapted for the ice, as she has been and is now used

Capt. Woolsey's Reminiscences 149

as a very successful boat in heavy ice. The *Swallow* and *Rochester* were opposition boats on the night line between New York and Albany, at that time landing all along the river, both leaving the same nights.

On April 7, 1845, a very dark and threatening night, the *Swallow* left Albany on her usual time with a goodly number of passengers and usual amount of freight. She had not proceeded far, when it set in to snow, the wind blowing heavy from the north and east, with every prospect and indication of its increasing to a gale. She had, by careful management of the pilot and captain, succeeded in getting to Coxsackie, where she landed, and she should have stayed there, for it proved to become darker, wind increasing to a gale, and the snow blinding the vision so that is was impossible to see anything ahead. I suppose the last object seen after leaving the narrow channel was the light on Four Mile Point. From that time it was all guess-work until she struck the Little Island Rock, which lay off the upper part of the then village of Athens, the pilot supposing that he was far enough down to shape his course to go through Pierce's Reach, below Athens, which course is much more to the west than the reach above. She must have been going at full speed, for her bow was completely out on the rock, her stern in deep water, which caused her to break in two just aft of the forward gangway. There was a number of passengers, about thirteen male, lost. It being a very cold, severe, northeast snow-storm there were more lost than if it had been warm weather.

The *Swallow* was a very nice boat for her day, not quite as long as the *Rochester*, her opponent, nor so low in the water. She had a large bird, a flying swallow, painted on her wheel-house. I remember the same gale did much damage all along the river, there being a number of vessels swamped. There was a very heavy swell in Newburgh bay. The sloop *Levant* was coming down the river loaded, and trying to make a harbor, sunk at the dock just below First

Street. The sloop *Rising Sun* also, in the same gale, laying to anchor off the lower part of the Hook Mountain, just above Nyack, started her anchors and dragged them below Nyack, went ashore and to pieces, drowning the captain and one man. Somehow, I do not think we now have such severe weather or gales, nor do they last so long as formerly.

About this time, or a little later, there was an incident or accident which happened on one of the up-trips of the *Rochester*. I remember, also, it was blowing heavy from the southeast, for I was at the Long Dock the same night she landed there. It was the custom in those days for all of the steamers to carry a good sized yawl-boat at or near the after gangway, where the passengers came aboard; this boat was carried on two heavy iron davits or cranes, with good, suitable threefold tackles attached to the cranes, there being a boat on both sides of the steamer, but for what purpose they were carried there, I cannot conceive, unless in case of accident, if a passenger should fall overboard to rescue him. It was the custom to have one man, expert in handling the boat, a good swimmer, reliable and fearless, selected from the crew, to take charge of the boat at every landing. When she was lowered into the water, the stern and bow-painters were passed around one of the guard-braces, the tackles unhooked, and so the boat was under the guard, aft of the wheel, while landing; the man in her holding the stern-painter tight, keeping the boat close to the hull of the steamer until she left the dock, then the tackles were hooked and the boat hoisted out of the water again. The man chosen for this purpose on the *Rochester* was Constantine Smith, whom I knew, he being the father of Captain Coleman's wife, also Captain Jacob DuBois' wife, so long on the old steamer *Norwich*. As I have said, when she landed that night it was blowing very heavy from the southeast and there was a strong flood-tide.

Capt. Woolsey's Reminiscences

I have always noticed in my experience on the river, that in a southeaster, the farther you go up the river, the stronger the wind blows. Also, in a northeaster when leaving Albany, the farther down the river you go, the stronger the wind blows—and so on this particular night when the *Rochester* reached Coxsackie it was blowing very heavy, which necessitated the steamer backing stronger than usual. Mr. Smith was in the small boat under the guard. There being an extra strain on the painters, they parted, which let the boat go under the wheel, ground up the boat and killed Mr. Smith. What there was left of him was found some time afterwards down at Four Mile Point. It was not long after this accident that the custom of carrying the boats in the gangway on davits was abolished. The *South America* was one of the steamers which has made the best time from New York to Albany. She came out just after the *Swallow* and *Rochester* on the night line between New York and Albany. She was still an improvement on the former boat, and very much so in respect to speed. Her run, stern and after part were much finer and sharper than any other boat which had been built, power greatly increased, so much so, that she made the fastest time from New York to Albany on record, which was something less than eight hours, I think, seven hours and forty-five minutes, making seven landings. Although I remember that the conditions were exceptionally favorable. She having a heavy southeast wind, also a strong flood-tide which she carried all the way through. In those days they did not observe running on schedule time as now, but went through as fast as possible, but this, as far as I know, is the fastest time on record, and in those days was frequently alluded to as the fastest time to Albany from New York.

The other boats which I have spoken of, that came out about that time, were the *Utica*, *Robert L. Stevens*, also the *Norwich*, which I think was built some little time before the others. However, they all were used as passenger and freight boats on the river until about the year 1850, and then used as tow-boats. The old *Norwich* running from Rondout, was owned by Thomas Cornell and the engineer, a Mr. Moore, who always was on her and ran the engine, he being a very kind, sociable man, and very attentive to his duties as an engineer. I remember that these three boats, the *Utica*, *Robert L. Stevens*, and *Norwich* in those days were used winters in the ice. The *Utica* always had a false bow put on, expressly for the ice. The other two, in the formation of their hulls and bows, were constructed in a manner so that they were a complete success as regards to fighting ice, and if their engines had the increased power which they give boats in these days, they would have been much more efficient in the ice. The Erie Railroad used all three of them, also the powerful Sandy Hook boats, *William Webb*, *New Haven*, and *Doctor Kane*, to keep the river open in the winter from Piermont to

New York. When the Erie was first constructed, their terminal was at Piermont, some twenty-two or twenty-three miles from the city. All of the freight and passengers from the West were transferred at this point on barges and steamers for New York, which necessitated much work, and very hard, dangerous work and navigation in the severe winters which we formerly had.

The river frequently, in those days, was packed full of heavy ice to the city. I have many times seen the harbor just as full of ice as any other portion of the river; in fact, I have seen people walking across both the East and North Rivers on the ice. Sometimes it would take two days to get to the city with these boats from Piermont. I have heard Captain Jacob DuBois say that at one time, in one of those severe winters, he was one week with the *Norwich* getting from Piermont to the city. I know, and am confident from what I have seen and from past experience, that we have not as severe winter weather as formerly, but if we did have now just as severe winters, the great advancement and improvements of this, our day, the wonderful accommodation and facilities for travel and transfer of freight of all kinds, which man has invented and sought out, I believe would overcome the severest winters that we ever had. During one or two of those winters of the forties, two of these boats, I remember, the *Utica* with her false bow, and the *Robert L. Stevens* attempted the experiment, and did form a daily line between Newburgh and New York, each coming up on alternate days. They succeeded very well in their endeavors, but it was hard work. The wear and severe strain on the wheels and boats in general, I think, caused it to be a failure financially. The winters were quite severe, the river being frozen from shore to shore, they having a track to come through, which they had to break through afresh every day, the same as our ferry boats do now when the ice is fast. I have seen the boys skating close alongside of them when coming up and often jump from the ice on the *Utica's* false bow, or on the *Robert L. Stevens*' guards.

Before I pass on to mention other steamers, I will notice one which I had nearly forgotten. I can just remember her as running a short time from Cornwall. I am sure that she did not run there long. It was the old steamboat *Experiment*, a Captain Griswold in charge of her. She ran from there as freight and passenger boat. Where she went to, or what became of her, I cannot say, for, about the year 1840, the sloop *Revenge*, Captain Joseph Ketcham, had the business, and it was at that time very successfully carried on by him, as he was a thorough business man. I think Reeve Ketcham, the lawyer, in Mr. Cassidy's office is his son. I remember also that Jesse Masten, so long pilot of the West Point ferry, was the mate and sailing master of the *Revenge*, and that he went from there to the ferry at West Point when they ferried with rowboats. About this time, 1838 or

1840, the steamboat *Emerald* was sunk just below Cornwall, in the cove between Butter Hill [1] and the Crow's Nest, but however, the circumstances of her filling I have forgotten. Then a few years later on they broke her shaft and ran her on the Two Brothers, a reef of rocks a little below West Point Foundry dock at Cold Spring, there also she filled. This was in the year 1845.

After the sad and fatal disaster of the *Neptune*, which occurred on November 24, 1824, there was a decisive feeling against sloop navigation, in respect to carrying passengers on the sloops and packets. Noticing that their business had fallen off in respect to passengers, and somewhat in freight also, in the following year there was a meeting called in January, of sloop owners and forwarders, to consider the situation. At the meeting there was a committee appointed to look into and report relative to the building of good and efficient steamboats for the purpose of

[1] Now called Storm King.—W. E. V.

carrying freight and passengers from the village of Newburgh and landings nearby. The chairman of that meeting was Selah Reeve, and David Crawford was secretary. The committee consisted of John P. De Wint, Uriah Lockwood, John Wiltse, Christopher Reeve and David Crawford.

In the winter of 1829 and 1830, Christopher Reeve bought the steamer *Baltimore* and placed her on the route to New York in the spring of 1830, and ran alternately, first from Reeve's dock, then from Crawford's dock. She, of course, was very rude and commonplace, as all of the first steamers were, yet she was hailed with a popular feeling and regard. The same year, (1830) the *William Young* which was being built at Low Point was launched. She commenced to run from Benjamin Carpenter's dock in September. She had much the same appearance as the *Baltimore*, as I saw both afterwards. Her owners claimed, however, that the *Young* was the better boat and a better model, and claimed her to be the fastest boat. The *Baltimore* continued to run from Newburgh until the year 1835, and then was transferred to the Albany route from Newburgh. Then came on the scene of action the steamers *Legislator* and *Providence*. In 1833 David Crawford built the steamer *Washington* and put her on the route in November of that year for the first; she was larger and superior to any which had been built. She created quite a competition and aroused the energies of the other freighting establishments, and caused Mr. Carpenter to build the *James Madison* in the year 1835, which was a boat in many points superior to the *Washington*, being very proud of having the first beam-engine on the river or in the carrying trade.

Mr. Crawford's business was so increased that he ran both the *Baltimore* and the *Washington* for a while. Then Thomas Powell built the steamer *Highlander* at Philadelphia. She, in her day, was first class, in many respects superior to her rivals, especially in speed. I remember her greatest rival in speed was the *Rochester* on the Albany and New York route. It is well known by some of our oldest citizens that there was so much said and such a feeling in respect to the speed of the two boats, that there was a bet made of $1000 to race from New York to Newburgh. The race came off, and the *Highlander* lost by half a minute, on a straight run. The *Osceola* was a neat little boat for her day and speedy, running between Poughkeepsie and New York, also on the morning line. They challenged the old *Highlander* and the old boat won, and so kept up her reputation. Up to the time that the *Thomas Powell* was built (1846) there were wonderful strides made in the speed of steamers on the river, but the progress since has not advanced in speed, only in comfort and convenience to the public.

The first five steamboats that were built for business on the Hudson River were the *Clermont, Robert Fulton, Fire-Fly, Paragon*

Capt. Woolsey's Reminiscences 163

and the *Lady Richmond*. These boats were built by Bell & Brown of New York City. These steamboats were owned by Robert Fulton and Robert L. Livingston, and at first, run by them. A Mr. Samuel Goodrich in those early days had one of the two shipyards at Coxsackie; Mr. Timothy Wood having the other. These steamers of Mr. Fulton's and Mr. Livingston's were frequently repaired at Mr. Goodrich's shipyard at Coxsackie. Mr. Goodrich afterwards removed to Hyde Park, where he established a shipyard and built the famous old steamer *Novelty*, carrying on an extensive business there. The construction of the *Novelty* was begun in the fall of 1830. Her keel was laid alongside of the little creek which flows down through the hills and empties into the Hudson, where the station of the Hudson River Railroad now stands, and when navigation opened in the spring of 1831 she was finished. In those days the method for getting lumber quickly and to order in the shape it was desired was not the same as it is now. Along the river was an abundance of all kinds of trees and of any size desired. The ship carpenter could go into the woods and select the keel, stem, sternpost and ship-knees, as he wished. This was done in the case of the *Novelty*. The engine was built at the Novelty Iron Works, New York City, whence her name. Her engine was neither cross-head nor walking-beam, but it was a horizontal incline engine. The secret of her great speed at that early day was the smart engine and the new style of boiler, altogether different and a new departure and invention which generated steam faster and of greater volume than the first old boilers in the former boats built.

This improved steamboat boiler was first the thought and invention of a man by the name of Bliss. Afterwards a Doctor Mott, a stove dealer, got hold of the patent, and it has ever since been called or known as the Tubular Boiler, but has been greatly improved on since. For this increased volume and pressure of steam the model of the *Novelty* was a little too fine; her hull was one hundred and seventy-five feet long; forward her designer had departed from the former style of full bow, therefore when under full pressure of steam she buried too much. This defect was remedied by the construction of a false bow, which overcame the difficulty and gave her the buoyancy of a duck. This false bow was thirty feet long, making her two hundred and five feet long. After her running a while and everything in working order, the *Novelty* went to Albany and made her memorable trip to New York, her time was seven hours and thirty-five minutes, including landings at Kinderhook, Coxsackie, Hudson, Catskill, Bristol, Red Hook, Kingston Point, Hyde Park, Poughkeepsie, Milton, Newburgh, West Point, Caldwell's, if the accounts are reliable. Faster time has been claimed by other boats, but this was a revolution in the speed of side-wheel boats back in the thirties, due to different model and the introduction of the tubular boiler in the *Novelty*, which has led to the coil boilers afterwards. The *Novelty* was not run long on the route to Albany, she having the advantage over the boats of the North River Steamboat Company. The history of the *Novelty* was ended on the North River, there being a contract made with the owner of the *Novelty* and owners of the other boats and she was taken off. But it must not be forgotten that all of the steamers coming after had tubular boilers. Mr. Samuel Goodrich built other boats and vessels at Hyde Park, viz., the barge *J. L. Rathbone*, sloop *Waterloo*, schooner *W. L. Ruff*, and the *Old Hickory* for people on Staten Island.

To show the longevity and usefulness of a well-built boat—in fact the vessels, steamers and barges which they built in my younger days are far superior to the wooden vessels of this day, all of our old craft have proved the truth of what I say— take the case of the barge *Minnisink* which was built at Milton by David Sands, and a more honest shipbuilder never lived, everything he did was done upon honor. Another fact also I have noticed in my long experience is, that the timbers formerly procured and used in my early days were much superior to the timbers and planking used now. The *Minnisink's* keel was laid in the year 1838, the frame was of the best of locust, white oak and red cedar. She was not finished until about 1840, so that her frame was allowed to season well while building; David Crawford of Newburgh then bought her for the freighting business. She was fully and completely fastened with bolts and washers riveted and locust treenails wedged. Her original length was one hundred and twenty-five feet, and in 1854 Crawford cut her in two and added thirty feet amidships, giving her a length of one hundred and fifty-five feet. She was fitted up the best for those days both for passengers and for freight. In 1856 Crawford & Company sold her to B. Carpenter & Company, and they in 1864 sold her to

Homer Ramsdell. In 1868 her planking was worn so thin by water and ice that Mr. Ramsdell replanked her and did other work necessary to place her in first-class condition. Mr. Ramsdell kept her steadily at work until 1872, when she was used as a spare boat and for excursions, and I believe she was then used as a receiving barge in New York, receiving all freight that was not disposed of by the other boats which ran daily, and if memory serves, she was kept by Mr. Ramsdell, usefully employed, until about the year 1879 or so, having been in use for some forty years for Newburgh people, and of late years she was used as a lighter around the harbor.

ADDITIONAL NOTES ON SLOOPS BY CAPTAIN
GEORGE D. WOOLSEY.

Sloop *Catharine*, Captain William Wandel, sailed from Daniel Smith's dock, 1800.

Sailed from Daniel Smith's dock, two miles above Newburgh, 1804, sloop *Confidence*, Captain Griggs.

SLOOP ''GENERAL PUTNAM,'' BUILT BY CHARLES COLLYER
From an oil painting

Capt. Woolsey's Reminiscences

Sloop *Sportsman*, Daniel T. Smith, captain, 1804, sailed first from Hugh Walsh's dock, after Daniel Smith's dock, two miles above Newburgh.

Samuel Seymour carried on the shipbuilding business at the foot of South Street, Newburgh, until the last of the year 1805. In the year 1804 he fell into the hold of a ship he was building for the West India trade, which accident caused him to be lame afterwards; the shipyard then came into possession of Timothy and Samuel Wood, brothers. Timothy removed to Coxsackie about 1812, built the *Timothy Wood* and the *Addison* about 1819, when there. Samuel Wood retained the yard at foot of South Street, where he built the *Argus, Meridian, Orange Packet, Illinois*, and other sloops, also the *Neptune* (1820), and the *Illinois* (1818).

In the year 1804, the sloop *Diligent*, Captain James Bloomer, was run as a packet from Walsh's dock, village of Newburgh, to New York, freight and passengers.

In the year 1803, the sloop *Amelia* was on the route from Newburgh to Albany.

In the year 1803, the sloops *Jefferson* and *Two Sisters* were run as packets to New York from Newburgh.

In the year 1803, the sloop *Fanny*, Captain Samuel Logan; also the *Orange* and sloop *Goliath* were packets to New York.

In the year 1803, the sloop *Belvidere*, Captain Leonard Carpenter, owner, and the sloop *Justice*, Captain John Helms ran on the line to New York.

In the year 1800, the sloops *Vice-President*, *Senator Burr*, and *Ceres* ran on the line to New York.

In the years 1804 and 1805, Jacob and Leonard Carpenter had the sloops *Mary* and *Sally Jane* on the line from the village of Newburgh to New York, running from their dock.

In the years 1800 and 1801, the sloops *Hopewell*, *Eliza Washington*, and *Minerva* were run from the village of Newburgh.

In 1802, the *Harriet*, *Goshen*, and *Katy*

Capt. Woolsey's Reminiscences 171

Maria were run from his dock, by Jacob Powell, at Newburgh.

Two years before, in the year 1800, he ran the sloop *Montgomery*, carrying passengers and freight.

On November 11, 1804, the sloop *Nelly Maria*, Captain Van Keuren of Poughkeepsie, upset opposite the village of Newburgh, in a heavy gale, all hands and passengers were rescued.

THE END

www.ingramcontent.com/pod-product-compliance
Lightning Source LLC
Chambersburg PA
CBHW050905300426
44111CB00010B/1380